Fixing our broken democracy

The case for 'Total Representation'

Ken Ritchie

Fixing our broken democracy
The case for 'Total Representation'

Foreword by Professor Tony Wright

Dr Ken Ritchie was Chief Executive of the Electoral Reform Society from 1997 to 2010. Prior to 1997, he held a number of senior positions in the voluntary sector, including UK Director of Practical Action, Deputy Director of the Refugee Council and Executive Director of Healthlink Worldwide. He contested the 1987, 1992 and 1997 general elections as a Labour candidate.

Professor Tony Wright is Visiting Professor of Government and Public Policy at University College, London. From 1992 until his retirement in 2010, he was Labour MP for Cannock Chase. As an MP he chaired the Select Committee on Public Administration for over a decade. He also chaired the Select Committee on Reform of the House of Commons – referred to as the 'Wright Committee' – which secured major reforms to the way in which the Commons works, in the wake of the parliamentary expenses scandal.

Fixing our broken democracy

The case for 'Total Representation'

Contents

PART 4: The way ahead

Appendices

Preface

Those who think that last year's AV referendum buried electoral reform for ever are likely to be disappointed. The referendum result was certainly a disaster for electoral reformers, but the real disaster was the process which produced this outcome. The referendum proposition did not derive from any inquiry into electoral systems, capable of producing a national conversation about what we want from an electoral system, but from an imposed political fix. Little wonder then that it came unstuck.

Next time it needs to be different. The reason for thinking that there will be a next time comes directly from the failure of the First Past the Post system to deliver single party majority government. This was the attribute above all others that was always offered as its supreme justification. If this has now gone, as seems to be the situation, then the case for sticking with the present system becomes much weaker. The argument is no longer that a new electoral system is needed in order to get a different kind of politics, but that precisely because we have a new kind of politics then a more appropriate kind of electoral system is needed for it.

But what kind of system? There is no perfect system, only different sorts of imperfection. But we could explore what we want an electoral system to do (the answers are less straightforward than they might seem), what there is to be learned from experience here and elsewhere, and how we might best secure the attributes we value. That requires inquiry, discussion and debate. Then we could have a proper referendum that grew out of this civic conversation.

That is why this book by Ken Ritchie is so welcome and timely. It makes the case for what he calls Total Representation, which combines the single member constituency system with an imaginative (and flexible) way to get additional members from the best losers. It is not necessary to sign up to the precise details of such a system to recognise that it makes an important and undogmatic contribution to thinking about what a desirable kind of electoral system might look like. It deserves to be widely read, and discussed. I hope it will generate the kind of informed debate on the issue that is now so badly – and urgently- needed.

Tony Wright

Introduction

If I had been asked to write this book ten, or even five, years ago I would have declined the invitation. In the decade that followed Labour's election victory in 1997 there was always a hope that Labour would honour its 1997 manifesto commitment to hold a referendum on how we elect our MPs, even if that hope gradually faded as the years passed. What Labour promised in 1997 was a chance to change to a 'broadly proportional' system and the Jenkins Commission, which it established within months of its election, recommended what it called 'the Alternative Vote Plus' (AV+). Although this was not a perfect system - reformers kept up the pressure for a more radical reform - AV+ had been put on the agenda and appeared to be the system for which those who wanted change would need to campaign.

Throughout these years, in my work with the Electoral Reform Society I wrote innumerable papers on what the ideal voting system should achieve, always ending with the conclusion that STV (the Single Transferable Vote) was the thing to aim for. I stand by the arguments I made, but what was missing was the sense of what was possible. The Society's work may have helped bring about a change to STV for Scottish local government elections, but there was never a chance that either of the two major parties would back it as a runner for general elections. Even if they had offered a referendum on STV, with the opposition of so many leading politicians it would have been a dead duck. As we found in 2011, even AV, without the small degree of proportionality that AV+ would have provided, could easily be shot down in the referendum the Liberal Democrats extracted from the Conservatives in their coalition deal: AV was, in the words of one observer, "an unwanted child of an unhappy marriage of convenience".

Electoral reform now needs a new project, and Aharon Nathan has provided one. The Total Representation (TR) system he has devised does not attempt to do everything that STV could do; it does not attempt to be radical; it softens the very negative features of FPTP without totally abandoning it. TR is therefore a system that offers electoral reformers a way forwards, while at the same time respecting the concerns of those who, for whatever reasons, are wary of change.

A major attraction of TR, however, is its simplicity. It is essentially a First-Past-the-Post election (the type we are all familiar with) in which the 'wasted' votes for losing candidates are used to make the outcome fairer to candidates and their parties and, most importantly, to voters. At a stroke it tackles two of FPTP's most serious defects - it corrects the very distorted outcomes that FPTP can produce and it makes more votes 'count' (in the sense that they help secure the election of an MP).

Making more votes count would on its own be sufficient reason for giving consideration to TR. My own appreciation of the need for a better voting system came from my experiences in the three general elections I have fought. In none was there ever a chance that I would win, but I diligently toured the streets telling people how important a vote for me could be. Of course it was nonsense. Even in 1997 when I gained over 22,000 votes – enough to win in many other constituencies – the result would have been exactly the same if all 22,000 had stayed at home, or even voted for my main opponent. With TR, these 22,000 votes might not have won a seat for me, but they would have mattered as they could have helped win a seat for my party, and I would have been able to argue their importance with sincerity. An alternative subtitle for this book might have been "How to stop wasting votes".

There will, however, be electoral reformers who dismiss this book as heresy. A few years ago I might have been one of them. There are some for whom STV is not just an objective but almost a religion, and others who respond to any proposed electoral system with detailed calculations of indices of proportionality: STV is of course a good voting system, and measures of proportionality have some, even if limited, value, but electoral reform must be about achieving change. I hope therefore that those who are serious about wanting a better democracy will be prepared to consider TR as a step worth taking.

In democratic politics progress is only made by finding ideas which can win broad support, and that may mean making compromises between what we want and what is achievable. Events of recent years make it clear that the majority of politicians at Westminster have no stomach for any radical change in our voting system, and that getting backing for radical change at Westminster, or for the opportunity to bring it about by winning a referendum, is a long way off. We may all have our visions of a perfect democracy, but electoral reform is a political process and politics is the sometimes messy and often frustrating art of the possible. The task of true reformers must therefore be to seek a way ahead around which a broad coalition of support can be built.

This book, however, has not just been written for electoral reformers. There are many good, intelligent people who know that our present voting system does not work well, but who have genuine concerns at alternatives that have been proposed. If they truly believe in the need for a more consensual form of politics, their views cannot simply be ignored – they cannot be regarded as the enemy just because they do not fully accept all our arguments. Instead we need to engage with them, openly debating differences in an atmosphere of mutual respect, and seeking proposals on which there is sufficient common agreement to make progress possible. I believe that TR is such a proposal.

I am an electoral reformer and I have described TR as an electoral reform. Some, however, might regard that as an overstatement given the relatively minor changes TR would make to our present First-Past-the-Post system. Modest though they might be, I am convinced that the changes TR would make are vitally important and that the case for TR is compelling. However, as TR seeks to improve rather than overthrow FPTP, I would be content if TR were described as 'electoral repair' rather than electoral reform.

The cause of electoral reform is far from dead. The defeat of AV in the 2011 referendum was a severe setback but it would be a mistake to assume that as a consequence we are stuck with FPTP for the foreseeable future. The next opportunity to try to change to voting system may come sooner than we expect, particularly with the trend we have seen from two-party to multi-party politics and the increased likelihood of hung parliaments it produces. When the opportunity arises, if it is to be taken then those who want change must unite behind a winnable proposition, and TR could be that proposition.

I am very grateful to Aharon Nathan for suggesting to me that I write this book, but I would not have done so if I did not believe in the potential of TR. Although he and I have had discussions at various stages during the writing, the views expressed and the recommendations on how TR might best be applied in the UK are mine and mine alone.

I am also grateful to Joshua Payne for his detailed proof-reading of the text and for his many helpful comments.

Ken Ritchie

July 2012

Fixing our broken democracy

PART 1

Why we must fix our democracy

CHAPTER 1

Unrepresentative democracy

"England is the mother of all parliaments" declared John Bright in 1865, and over the years Bright's assertion has allowed us to extol the virtues of British democracy in a way that must make Bright, who was a radical reformer, turn in his grave. He did, however, have a point. We can trace the origins of our Commons back to 1264 when Simon de Montfort asked counties and boroughs to send two representatives, with the requirement that they should be elected, to form his parliament. It was, of course, far from representative democracy as we know it today, and it did not last long – Henry III was not keen on this challenge to his authority and De Montfort was slain in battle the following year. Seeds had, however, been sown, although it would take them centuries to germinate. The struggle for democracy is full of heroic stories of ordinary people who lost their liberty, and even their lives, for political freedoms and rights. It was not until the nineteenth century, with the demands of the Chartists and others, that our parliamentary democracy developed into

15

anything like its present form, and it was not until 1918 that the right to vote was extended to women – and it was another 10 years before women, like men, could vote at the age of 21. Universal adult suffrage was something that people had struggled and suffered for over many years and its achievement was something to be celebrated but, alas, in other respects the democracy people fought for is not what they got.

This book proposes a simple change to our voting system – not one that would produce a perfect democracy (whatever that might mean) and not one that would produce perfect politicians, but one that would get us nearer to the sort of democracy we need for the twenty-first century.

Democracy itself is, of course, much older than that British, or even the English, parliament. The Greeks were at it about 500 years before the birth of Christ. Theirs was, however, 'direct democracy' – in each city-state people, as long as they were not women or slaves, could meet together to take part in debates and vote on the issues under discussion. While that was possible in single city-states, which by present day standards were very small ones, it cannot be done with nation states and electorates numbering in the millions. We therefore must make do with 'representative democracy': we choose those who will represent us in debates and vote on our behalf.

That at least is the theory. But what if those we elect do not really represent us? That can happen if we do not get the voting system right – we may find ourselves with a parliament that does not reflect the way people voted, a government that most people don't want, and policies that most people oppose and, alas, in Britain that's a situation in which we have often found ourselves.

There will, of course, be issues on which there is not majority support for any course of action and no reasonable person would expect their government to please all of the people all of the time - even pleasing most for most of the time might be a tall order. But we should be able to expect a government that is respected and whose authority to take decisions, and even unpopular decisions, is recognised and accepted – a government that will at least take account of the balance of public opinion on any issue and that will act in the interests of "the many and not the few" (to use a bit of New Labour-speak). It is, however, a long time since Britain has had a government that enjoyed widespread trust and respect. In an opinion poll in 2010[1] four people in ten said they "almost never" trusted the government to put the national interest first, and in another poll[2] 72% agreed that "The present voting system produces governments which do not represent the views of most ordinary people", while only 11% disagreed. People may have responded to the question on the basis only of their perceptions, but in chapter 2 we will look at the facts and show that, at least in this second poll, the majority had good reasons for believing their government does not represent them. With our present voting system we have a very defective form of representative democracy.

Our MPs should be our agents at Westminster, representing our interests and accountable to us. They cannot of course support all the conflicting views of their constituents, but in a healthy

---

[1] British Social Attitudes Survey, Dec 2010
[2] State of the Nation Survey, 2010, ICM for Joseph Rowntree Reform Trust

democracy we should at least expect our politicians to command respect as people working for the broad, collective interests of their constituents and the country at large. Instead, however, we regard our politicians with suspicion, and indeed derision.

People have never trusted politicians, and a certain amount of healthy scepticism of the motives of those seeking political office is perhaps good. But scepticism has changed to cynicism, and cynicism to contempt. According to a poll in 2011, only 14% of us generally trust MPs to tell the truth and 80% do not.[3]

The misdemeanours of some MPs over the years can only have exacerbated this sense of distrust. In the 1990s we had the 'cash-for-questions' scandal; in 2007 and 2008 we had the 'cash-for-honours' allegations; and in 2009 it emerged that many had been abusing the system of parliamentary expenses – in some cases to the extent that MPs ended up behind bars (the pollsters tell us that the effect on trust was only slight, perhaps suggesting that such behaviour was only what people expected). In 2011 it emerged that a cabinet minister had toured the world on our behalf with an unofficial 'advisor' acting for business and American right-wing interests, and in 2012 the Leveson inquiry has thrown a light on the seedy relationships between some senior politicians and the media. However, the roots of distrust go much deeper than the actions of individuals. Although most MPs are decent people who want to work in the public interest (even if they have strange and sometimes misguided ideas about what that is), they suffer from being members of a parliament that lacks democratic legitimacy and therefore respect. The

---

[3] Ipsos Mori Veracity Index, 2011

problem lies, at least in part, in the way our voting system measures public opinion and coverts it into parliamentary seats.

It would be foolish to assume that there is any single remedy for malaise of British democracy, but unless we have elections that lead to parliaments in which the views of all significant groups of electors are fairly represented, in which issues can be debated in a reasoned manner, and which produce governments that are perceived as having the legitimacy to govern, we will not overcome the problem. We can't have true representative democracy without a voting system that gives us broadly representative parliaments.

This book is about a simple change we can make to our voting system – a change that would go some way to giving us a parliament that better reflects that range of opinions within the electorate and a government that commands more public trust.

Now's the time for reform

Why now? Many will argue that this is not the time for tinkering with our electoral arrangements: we are facing the worst economic crisis we have seen since the days of the Great Depression and dealing with that crisis must be the priority. As a result of the greed and recklessness of the elite of the banking community, many people are facing unemployment, threats to their savings and cuts in the services on which they depend. It is not just companies that are going to the wall, but several European countries are close to insolvency with implications for all western economies. Our attention, they argue, should be focused on finding economic solutions.

Of course the economic problems must be addressed, and urgently. But the crisis is not just one of economics – it is also one of politics. We are not facing a natural disaster but one that has arisen from the way countries have managed, or failed to manage, their affairs. It may have been created by the bankers, but why did the politicians allow it to happen? Fearful of bankers' power, politicians of all parties argued for only 'light touch' regulation of financial markets rather than intervening to safeguard the interests of ordinary people. And now that we're in this mess, are the politicians really in control of the situation? Millions of pounds of our money have been used to rescue banks from the consequences of their own folly but, in spite of politicians' protestations, top bankers continue to award themselves bonuses that many of their customers could not earn in decades. As Jeffery Sachs has put it:

> "in the face of high unemployment, growing inequality and looming government deficits, most governments are paralysed, in thrall to powerful interests. Wall Street, the City of London and Frankfurt banks and other corporate lobbies hold politics in their grip, and block effective change".[4]

What we are witnessing is a failure of politics. It is inevitable that at times like this people's confidence in politics and politicians will be shaken. Politicians failed to foresee the approaching storm and now they must ask ordinary people to pay the cost. Although we have not in Britain seen the violent demonstrations that have rocked some other countries in Europe, we have seen protests in our streets and many manifestations of public anger.

---

[4] Guardian, 17 December 2011

It is not just the authority of the government that is being challenged, but the competence of our democratic system in responding effectively and fairly to the problems that confront the nation. Austerity measures will never be popular, but they are only likely to be palatable if they are seen to come from a government that has a strong democratic mandate and is perceived to be acting on behalf of the population at large.

In a democracy it cannot of course be guaranteed that the electorate will have a clear preference for one policy over another. In the first half of 2012, for example, the people of Greece have gone to the polls twice, confronted with the choice of accepting the EU's demands that Greece cuts it budget with all the hardship that would entail, or of defying the EU and going for a less severe alternative but with less certainty over how government services would be funded. Their second election, by the slenderest of margins, produced a coalition prepared to accept the EU prescription. A different electoral system, however, might have produced a different outcome with consequences for not just Greece but the whole of the EU – a clear demonstration of the importance of getting the right electoral arrangements.

Four years earlier the spotlight was on Iceland where financial blunders left the country teetering on the verge of bankruptcy. There, however, a silver lining was a realisation that the parliament responsible for debacle was not truly representative of Iceland's electors, leading to plans for a new constitution with a new electoral system – a recognition that economic and political reform must go hand-in-hand.

Britain's economic crisis has not reached the proportions of Greece or Iceland, but at present a majority of people do not see the government as the government they wanted, and it is not the government they voted for. While dealing with our economic problems cannot wait for democracy to be mended, acceptance that there is a democratic deficit and a plan to tackle it would go a long way in diffusing dissent and division in society.

The conflict between democracy and economic power is not a new one. What is new, however, is the extent to which the shape of the world appears to be being determined by bankers and big business rather than by people, elected by us as our representatives to act on our behalf. Indeed, some of our politicians seem closer to the financial elite than to the constituents whose interests they are supposed to be defending. If we are to find a way out of our present difficulties that leads to a fairer and better society, we will not just need economic remedies but a change in the nature of our politics.

This book does not offer any economic prescriptions, and it does not even offer the complete package of measures needed to make politics what it should be – the way that people collectively take decisions on the type of society they want to live in. But it offers a simple change in our voting system that would make government more representative of voters and give people more voice in the how our country is run.

We cannot, of course, guarantee that a more representative government would do any better in steering us out of crisis but, when big decisions have to be taken, it is vital that those taking them have, and are perceived to have, the democratic legitimacy to do so on our behalf. Where we strike the balance between prioritising debt reduction and stimulating growth involves much technical analysis of issues on which there is no consensus of expert opinion: the judgment to be made is as much political as economic and it is therefore important that it is made by those with a strong democratic mandate to do so. This is a time when politics must re-assert itself, and never has getting our political arrangements right been more important.

But has electoral reform not been rejected?

In a referendum in May 2011 the electorate decisively rejected a proposal to change the way we elect our MPs. Only 32% supported change while 68% opposed it. The aftermath of such a devastating defeat for reformers is surely, some might argue, not the time for trying again to change the voting system.

The referendum outcome was certainly a setback, but let's get it into context. Back in 1997 Labour was elected with a manifesto that promised a referendum on a "broadly proportional system" but, with a huge majority of seats, it had little inclination to change the system that had been so kind to it. Years of campaigning managed to do no more than keep the issue on the fringes of the political agenda until 2009 when Labour's leaders recognised that its days in government might be numbered and support for reform might be in its interests. However, with strong resistance to change within Labour's ranks, the most they offered in their 2010 manifesto was a referendum on the Alternative Vote (AV), the least radical reform they could think of at the time.

Labour, however, did not win in 2010. In the negotiations which followed the election of a hung parliament, the Conservatives found it necessary to concede the same referendum – although they opposed AV – as the price of support from the Liberal Democrats. What had started as a Labour project ended up as one of the coalition government, with the major coalition partner firmly against a 'yes' vote.

When it came to the referendum, the dice were stacked against success. With the Conservatives backing the 'no' campaign and Labour divided on the issue, the only party enthusiastic about AV was the Liberal Democrats but, and as a result of their support for a service-cutting government and their about-turn on the question of increased university tuition fees, Liberal Democrat support plummeted in the year that followed the 2010 election. For many Labour supporters, voting against what they saw as Nick Clegg's project was a good enough reason for voting against AV.

To make matters worse, the 'yes' campaign was abysmal. It failed to get across the message that the existing 'First-Past-the-Post' (FPTP) system was failing politics and had to be changed. It produced leaflets with claims that did not resonate with voters' concerns and did not even convince its own activists – such as AV being a system that would make MPs work harder. It squandered resources on ineffective local campaigns rather than making full use of the freepost delivery to voters that was on offer, and it failed to make effective use of the leading Labour politicians who might have persuaded more Labour supporters of the benefits of change. By contrast the 'no' campaign was effective and well-managed, even if lacking in honesty on occasions. Its claim, for example, that a change to AV would cost so much that there would be cuts in health and other services was nonsense, and they knew it, but it was effective. Similarly the claim that AV would advantage the BNP helped swing people against reform, although it was clear that AV is a system that would have made chances of the BNP winning seats even more remote.

Another problem for the 'yes' campaign was the product itself. Prior to the 2010 election, Nick Clegg had described AV as "a miserable little compromise" and that is how many of the campaign's supporters saw it. It would certainly have been an improvement over the existing FPTP system, but a very modest one; it would not have guaranteed fairer election results; it would not have got rid of safe seats; and it would not have changed politics in the way the 'yes' camp claimed. AV has merits, but it had not sufficient merits to convince the electorate of the case for change.

A defeat by a margin of 2:1 can never be good, but it was not the argument that FPTP was defective and must go that was defeated (in the debates around the referendum that argument was hardly even put before the voters). What was lost was a badly-presented case for "a miserable little compromise" in circumstances in which many electors were prepared to vote against the AV's main proposers rather than the proposal itself. When we consider:

- the inadequacy of the change that was on offer,
- the failures of the 'yes' campaign,
- the effectiveness of the 'no' campaign, and
- the prevailing hostility towards the main proponents, the Liberal Democrats,

it is some consolation that 33% of voters nevertheless voted 'yes'. The result demonstrates that there is an appetite for change and that another referendum on a better system, supported by a much better campaign in more favourable circumstances could win.

Prospects for reform

If our MPs dressed more casually, we would probably have seen some 'Been there, done away with that' T-shirts under the satisfied grins of the many politicians who were more than happy to see the defeat of AV. Throughout the years of Labour government there was always the outside chance that there would be a referendum which would shake up politics and, for those with an interest in maintaining the status quo, the inconclusive election result of 2010 and the referendum deal was a real threat. It may appear to some that the defeat of AV in the referendum has removed that threat and knocked electoral reform off the agenda for years to come.

The situation for reformers is certainly not ideal. They fought a battle and lost, and, even if they fought the battle against the odds, on the wrong turf, inadequately equipped and poorly led, losing was not the outcome they wanted. With their energies dissipated and their money spent, there is an air of demoralisation in the reform camp.

This, however, is not the time for defeatism. Never has the need for a better and more representative democracy been greater and, even if the situation looks gloomy, it is far from as bad as it appears. On the positive side, let's firstly remember that in spite of all of the deficiencies of the AV campaign, 6.1 million people voted for a change from FPTP. Secondly, our politics are getting more pluralist: the 2010 general election produced a hung parliament and it's odds on that FPTP will produce others and further opportunities for electoral reform to be put on the agenda. Thirdly, a consequence of this greater pluralism is that the defects of FPTP are likely to become more and more apparent. Finally, let's remember that the movement for electoral reform got underway a century and a half ago (the Electoral Reform Society was formed in 1884) – over these years it has suffered many disappointments and defeats, but the case for electoral reform has always been there and the movement has always bounced back.

Nevertheless, lessons must be learnt from the AV referendum. A new campaign will require a better strategy, more convincing messages to win the arguments and a campaign structure that can deliver success. Above all, however, it will need a proposal for change that can win broad political support, that can easily be explained and sold to the voting public, and that can guarantee to make a difference, even if not to the extent that reformers might want.   This book argues that 'Total Representation' (TR) could be that better system, and that the opportunity to put it before the electorate in a referendum might not be as far off as some think.

The UN Declaration on Human Rights asserts that: "The will of the people shall be the basis of the authority of government". England may have been 'the mother of all parliaments', but the UK has some way to go in achieving a parliament that adequately reflects the people's will. Whatever other problems beset the nation, electoral reform must not therefore be, as some have claimed, a matter just for chattering classes divorced from current difficulties, but part and parcel of the change we need to make if we are to emerge as a better society and one that is more in control of its own destiny.

CHAPTER 2

What's wrong with our voting system

Distorted representation

About a couple of weeks before the 2010 general election a YouGov opinion poll[5] found that voting intentions were:

Conservative	31%
Labour	26%
Liberal Democrat	34%
Other	9%

Astonishing although these figures were, they were not out-of-line with other surveys that showed the Liberal Democrats neck-to-neck with the Conservatives and Labour trailing badly. For a moment it looked as if a party that had been an 'also-ran' in all elections for almost a century was leading in terms of popular support. It appeared that their vote might increase by more than 50% from the 22% they won in 2005. When it came to the election, however, their vote did increase, but only from 22% to 23%.

Suppose, however, that in the election people had voted as the YouGov poll had predicted two weeks earlier. Would the Liberal Democrats have won, at least in the sense of being the largest party? Far from it. The party with most votes would have ended

---

[5] YouGov poll for The Sun, with fieldwork on 19th and 20th April 2010.

up in third place. We cannot accurately predict what the YouGov figures would have meant in terms of seats, but if we assume uniform swings across the country,[6] the seats won might have looked something like this:

Conservative	236
Labour	205
Liberal Democrat	178

Why the apparent surge of support for the Liberal Democrats evaporated when it came to election day is something for others to analyse, but if the support measured beforehand by YouGov had held up until the election, we would have had the most bizarre result that British politics had ever seen. In 1951 and first of the 1974 elections the party with most votes came second in terms of seats, but for what should have been the winning party to come a miserable third would have made a mockery of the idea that Britain is a representative democracy. It might, however, have been an outcome that put the final nails in the coffin of FPTP.

Although the actual 2010 results were not nearly as distorted as they might have been, there were nevertheless huge differences between parties' shares of the seats and their shares of the votes:

	Percentage vote	Percentage seats
Conservative	36.1	47.2
Labour	29.0	39.7
Lib Democrat	23.0	8.8
Other	11.9	4.3

---

[6] Swings are never uniform, but this is an adequate assumption to illustrate the point.

The Conservatives and Labour both won many more seats that their vote shares suggest they should have won, while the Liberal Democrats, as in previous elections, got nowhere near to the number of seats they might have expected. Other parties have even more reason to be annoyed: UKIP, for example, won 919,546 votes but did not win a single seat.

These 2010 results just follow the pattern of previous general elections. Winners often end up with exaggerated majorities (like Labour's 2005 majority of 80 over all other parties combined when it only had 35% of the votes), but on occasions the party with most votes is not the party with most seats – we get "wrong winners".

The reason that FPTP can produce such odd results is that it takes no account of votes cast for losing candidates: whether a constituency is won by a large margin or by a very slender majority makes no difference to the outcome in terms of seats. With FPTP elections are not won just on how many votes are cast, but where they are cast. Consider a simple example in which three parties, A, B and C, contest 5 constituencies with 100 voters in each. Suppose the votes cast were:

Constituency	A	B	C
1	40	35	25
2	40	35	25
3	40	35	25
4	40	35	25
5	20	50	30
Total	180	190	130

Here A wins the election with 4 seats to B's one. Party B received more votes than A, but B's votes are distributed in a way that only gives it a single seat. Party C has over a quarter of the votes, but as its support is evenly spread across all constituencies it does not have enough support in any constituency to win a seat. This is of course an extreme example to illustrate the point, but it is this effect that is largely responsible for FPTP's erratic behaviour. In 2005 Labour was efficient, like party A in our example, in converting votes into seats, allowing it to win a majority of seats with barely a third of the votes, while the Liberal Democrats (as well as parties such as UKIP) suffer the fate of party C with a lot of votes cast for losing candidates and for which they get no advantage.

Following the 2010 election, David Cameron's Conservatives have tried to make FPTP fairer by seeking constituencies that are nearly equal in size, but our example shows that even having exactly the same number of voters in each constituency does not solve the problem: as Shakespeare might have remarked, "The fault, dear David, lies not in our boundaries but in our voting system".

Regional disparities

FPTP's quixotic conversion of votes into seats is not just a problem at national level – when we look at regional results the picture is much worse. Even in its good years, the Conservatives struggle to win seats in Scotland, Wales and the North of England, while Labour is always hopelessly under-represented in the South-East. In Tony Blair's 'landslide' win of 1997 (on a mere 43% of the votes), the Conservatives won no seats in Scotland and Wales, but Labour only won just over a quarter of the seats in the South East. Although the Conservatives emerged as the largest party in 2010, they won only one of the 59 seats in Scotland, while Labour won only two of the 58 seats in Eastern England – figures which do not reflect Labour and Conservative support in these areas.

These regional distortions are not just bad for overall representation, but they are bad for government. The government at Westminster is the government of all of the UK, but it is led by a party with only one MP who represents a Scottish constituency. Concerns that the government will not be sufficiently responsive to Scottish issues are inevitable, and the people of Scotland could be forgiven for thinking that they have a UK government led by a party which they emphatically rejected and in which they have little influence. However, although the Conservatives won only about one sixtieth of the seats in Scotland, they received a sixth of the votes.

Safe seats

Most seats in general elections are 'safe' in the sense that there is one party whose support in a constituency has in past elections been so strong that the chances of that party's candidate not winning are remote. David Cameron's Witney seat has been Conservative for a century, and there was probably more chance of Cameron being struck by lightning on election day than him losing. In recent elections the Electoral Reform Society has been able to write confidently to candidates in about 70 – 75% of constituencies congratulating them on their victories before the campaign has even begun.

Those who are selected as candidates by the dominant parties in safe seats are almost being offered jobs for life. For them, the real election was the party selection contest – a process only involving a tiny proportion of people in the constituency – as they can expect to win and win again unless they are exposed as criminals or sexual deviants. The danger here is that with such job security, accountability to the wider electorate can suffer.

We cannot object to constituencies returning candidates of the same party election after election if there is a strong majority favouring that party and we cannot blame candidates for being successful. However, what is a problem with safe seats under FPTP is their effect on elections and electors. General elections in Britain are not general in the sense that they are fought equally across the country. With most seats safe, parties focus their campaigning resources on to the marginal constituencies – both those where they know they will need to fight hard to retain a seat and those where they see a chance of taking a seat from a rival. It is the marginals that are visited by cabinet and shadow cabinet members, that see the billboard campaigns, and in which electors see more canvassers and receive more leaflets than perhaps they would like. While there is an election campaign of some sort in every constituency (particular where the aim is building support for local council candidates), party campaign managers will effectively ignore safe seats and party activists from these constituencies will be encouraged to cross to marginals where their efforts could be more rewarding. No-hope candidates in safe seats must do their best to maintain the pretence that they are engaged in a real contest, and they may even enjoy a few weeks in the local limelight, but retaining their deposits and avoiding embarrassing mistakes is as much as their parties want from them.

Not only do parties have little incentive to campaign in safe seats, but electors have less incentive to vote. If you know who is going to win, why miss a favourite TV programme or a round of drinks at the pub to cast a seemingly worthless vote? If the candidate you support is clearly going to be a loser, your vote may not be totally meaningless – you may want to demonstrate support for your party and you may want to see your candidate doing as well as possible – but your vote will not make any difference to what matters, and that is who wins the seat. And if you are in the more fortunate position of knowing that your candidate will be a winner, your vote may add to a majority and the satisfaction candidates derive from them, but it is not critical in the way it might be in a marginal seat.

In the 2005 general election campaign it was reported that Labour and the Conservatives were targeting only 2% of electors. With FPTP this made sense. If 20% of constituencies were considered marginal (the number was probably less) and if in each marginal constituency 10% of electors were 'swing voters', then these swing voters on whom the outcome of the election was likely to depend were only 2% of the electorate. Elections that take the votes of most people for granted and whose outcomes depend on what a minority of voters do in a minority of seats cannot be good for democracy, but it is a consequence of FPTP.

Wasted votes

With FPTP there are no prizes for coming second: it's a case of 'winner takes all' and votes cast for candidates who are not winners might as well never have been cast – they are wasted votes.

FPTP is good at wasting votes, and it's getting better. Half a century ago when elections were essentially two-party contests, one candidate would get more than half the votes and would win, while the other would get less and lose, making the number of 'wasted' votes less than half of the total (although it was never quite as straightforwards as there have always been candidates from minor parties taking some of the votes). However, now that we are no longer a two-party system, candidates do not need 50% of the votes to win. Indeed, in the 2010 general election, only 38% of winners passed the 50% mark (and that was an improvement on 34% in 2005): in the Norwich South constituency the winner had only 29% of the votes and 71% were wasted on losing candidates. In the 2010 general election more than half (52.8%) of the votes cast were 'wasted' in this way.

It is worth noting here that because with FPTP a candidate does not need a majority of the votes to win, the winner can be the most unpopular candidate. In Hertfordshire in 2009, for example, the BNP won the South Oxley ward with only 29% of the votes when opinion polling suggested most voters would have wanted any candidate other than that of the BNP to win.

Some will argue that it is unfair to regard any vote for a losing candidate as wasted – not every candidate can win and there will also be votes cast for losers. That is partly true, but there are other voting systems (which we will consider in later chapters) that don't simply ignore the votes cast for losing candidates – systems in which all votes cast, even in safe seats, are used in some way in determining the overall election result. But the winner-takes-all nature of FPTP puts it at the top of the league as a vote waster. [7]

What we need to change

Distorted results and their consequent unfairness (particularly to significant minority parties), the focus of elections to swing voters in marginal constituencies, and the number of wasted votes that might as well never have been cast are three major problems of FPTP. Of course there are others, such as:

- The way in which FPTP encourages tactical voting – voting for the candidate most likely to defeat the candidate you don't want rather than for the candidate you really want;
- The adversarial nature of the politics produced by FPTP – because candidates don't need a majority of the votes but only more votes than any rival, it can be easier to win through negative campaigning, attacking opponents rather than a positive presentation of what candidates stand for and why;
- The difficulties FPTP raises to progress towards a better gender balance in parliament - as FPTP requires constituency parties to select only one candidate, too often

---

[7] Some also argue that votes for a winner that merely add to the winner's majority are also wasted as they do not affect the result. However, voters whose candidates win healthy majorities are unlikely to feel the pain of those who back a loser, so here we will regard only votes for losers as being wasted.

it is men, who are likely to have had more experience as party activists and who are less discouraged by the macho nature of FPTP politics, who are selected.

However, to overcome all problems of FPTP would require a quite radical reform, but reducing the extent to which election outcomes can be distorted, allowing significant minorities a voice in parliament, making election campaigns worth fighting in safe seats, and reducing the number of wasted votes are all things we can achieve with a simple change in the voting system. That takes us to the next chapter – Total Representation.

Part 2: 'Total Representation'

CHAPTER 3

Total Representation - the basics

This chapter explains what Total Representation (TR) is, how it works, and what it could do for our democracy. However, why TR should now be on the political agenda will be clearer if we begin by looking at where TR has come from and the problems it seeks to address.

The background

TR is the brainchild of Aharon Nathan. Most writings on voting systems come from politicians, political commentators, political scientists and social-choice theorists: professionally, Aharon Nathan falls into none of these categories, but in other ways he belongs to them all. He is someone whose whole life has been shaped by politics. He was born in 1931 in Iraq and spent his childhood with his Jewish family in Baghdad. The creation of Israel and the Arab-Israeli Conflict that ensued forced his family together with almost the entire Jewish community to move to Israel. While still in his early twenties he was appointed Senior Assistant Advisor on Arab affairs to Prime Ministers Ben Gurion and Moshe Sharett and, in the months that followed the Suez war, he set up and headed the first civil administration in the Gaza Strip. Since the 1960s he has lived in Britain where he studied social anthropology at Oxford and where he has had a successful career in business, but he has retained strong links with and worked on Arab Affairs closely with the directors general of the Prime Minister's Office first with Teddy Kollek and later on with Yaacov Herzog. In 2005 the Israeli President appointed him to a commission to look at the country's governance, and since that time he has been a board member of the Citizens' Empowerment Centre in Tel Aviv. Aharon Nathan's ideas on democracy are not therefore just the result of academic discussion but are the product of his deep concerns for the problems of the Middle East and his personal involvement in the quest for solutions.

Israel as a country is unique. Born out of centuries of anti-Jewish discrimination and the horrors of the holocaust, it is little more than half a century old. Its founding fathers wanted a secure homeland for Jewish people, but the resulting conflict and enmity drove hundreds of thousand Palestinians from their homes and made enemies of all the Arab neighbours. The rest, as they say, is history.

Israel's population may be relatively small (just under 8 million), but it is hugely diverse. The Jewish majority has people who originate from all parts of the Jewish Diaspora - people from Western societies, from Eastern Europe and many from the Arab world and even Africa – and although this majority may be united by its Jewish identity, there are big divisions over religious observance and the role that religion plays in society. Then there are the Arabs – Palestinians, and of course their descendants, who did not leave their homes in 1948. Attitudes to the peace process, the occupation of Arab lands and the treatment of the Palestinians, have all created major divisions not just between Jews and the non-Jewish Arabs, but also within the Jewish community itself. The unity Israel has achieved may be largely due to a common sense of isolation in the Arab Middle East and the perceived threat to its very existence.

Israel has, however, ensured that all parts of this heterogeneous society are represented in its parliament, the Knesset, by using an ultra-proportional voting system. It is a list system, similar to that used in Britain for European Parliament elections, but in Israel the entire country is treated as a single electoral region of 120 seats. This makes it easy for small parties to gain representation – there is a threshold they must pass to win a seat, but it is only 2%. As a result, the 2009 general election produced a parliament with 12 parties, none of them having as much as a quarter of the votes or seats. Forming a government therefore requires much horse-trading between several disparate groups – small parties can insist that their (sometimes idiosyncratic) concerns are addressed in government policy as the price of support for a coalition. It is not a process likely to provide a stable government with a clear mandate.

The list system also has the defect of Britain's European Parliament elections: voters cannot choose the candidates they want – only a party list. If a party wins 5 seats, then these are taken by the top 5 on that party's list, irrespective of their popularity. Candidates at the top of their party lists will be elected if their parties reach the 2% threshold, even if the voters regard them as being of little merit. On the other hand, candidates well-liked by their parties' supporters will not be elected if the parties put them too far down the list.

Consequently the accountability of Knesset members to groups of electors is limited.

For many years Aharon Nathan has been campaigning for a change in Israel's voting system. As part-Israeli but with his origins in the Arab world, he belongs to that important minority in Israel that wants a sensible dialogue between reasonable people on either side of the Israeli-Palestinian conflict. He sees the voting system and the style of politics it produces as making it more difficult for Israel to form a government that can effectively negotiate with Israel's Arab neighbours, as well as tackling the growing number of domestic problems in Israel itself.

What he has proposed is a move from Israel's ultra-proportional system. While sufficient proportionality to ensure that all significant groups in society have representation is good, a system that gives seats to any party that merely passes the 2% threshold can fracture the make-up of parliament to the extent that forming a government may involve backroom deals to meet the demands, and therefore gain the support, of very unrepresentative groups. Coalitions, in which parties must come together and agree a joint programme for government, are not necessarily bad – we will argue in chapter 5 that they can be good – but when coalitions involve several parties, not only do they become less stable (as smaller members can threaten to withdraw if they do not get their way), but resultant programmes can be very far from what people voted for. Proportionality is a desirable feature of an electoral system but, perversely, too much can undermine democracy by making post-election deals more important than what voters wanted.

For Aharon Nathan the system used in Britain, his adopted homeland, therefore had some attractions. The use of constituencies increases the accountability of MPs, it does not produce a plethora of minor parties with particular interests but encourages support for the major parties that can amalgamate views into a more realistic government programme, and even in years such as 2010 when elections led to hung parliaments the coalition options were narrower and clearer. However, Aharon Nathan, also aware of the hugely disproportional results FPTP can produce, has sought a system that builds on FPTP but goes some way to correcting its unfairness. Thus while Britain and Israel are at opposite ends of the spectrum in terms of proportionality, Aharon Nathan's prescription - TR – offers a compromise that could resolve, or at least ameliorate, many of the problems of both countries.

TR – how it works

TR, just like FPTP, is based on constituencies each of which elects a single MP. Like FPTP, the person elected in each constituency is the candidate with most votes. Both FPTP and TR use identical ballot papers and with both voters are required to put only a single 'X' against their preferred candidates. No-one can therefore argue, as they did with AV (even if rather disingenuously), that TR is too complicated.

As we have seen in chapter 2, however, major defects of FPTP, however, are:

- That it can produce very distorted results; and
- That many votes are cast for losing candidates (and consequently they do not contribute to the outcome);

- That in many constituencies that are 'safe' for one party or another, there is little incentive for supporters of other parties to vote.

TR corrects, at least in part, the distortions of FPTP by also electing what Aharon Nathan calls 'Party Members' to compensate. These members are elected by taking account of votes cast for losing constituency candidates, thereby overcoming the problem of large numbers of wasted votes, and by doing so the system gives all voters an incentive to vote (and to vote sincerely, i.e. for the candidate of the party they really want) even if they are in constituencies in which their preferred candidates have little hope of success.

The votes for losing constituency candidates are pooled and party seats awarded to parties on the basis of their share of these votes. For Israel, with its 120 seats, Aharon Nathan proposes that votes for losing candidates across the whole country are pooled to decide how the party seats should be allocated to parties, but for Britain, with its much larger parliament and electorate, pooling them at regional level may be a better option. Aharon Nathan has proposed they be allocated proportionally using the 'largest remainder' method (which is described in chapter 4 along with other possible methods that could be used).

If a party gains, say, 3 party seats, then they will be given to that party's three losing constituency candidates who got most support. 'Most support' could be decided on either the number of votes or the percentage of the votes they received – if constituencies are of roughly equal sizes, there will be little difference between the two approaches.

The greater the ratio of party seats to constituencies, the more proportional the system will be. Aharon Nathan proposes 1:4 for national parliaments to produce a system that is not fully proportional but which avoids excessive disproportionality and retains constituency elections as the predominant route to parliament. For second chamber elections, where a greater degree of proportionality might be desirable and the arguments for constituency representation weaker, he proposes 2:1. The ratio, however, can be adjusted according to taste.

A simple example

Suppose four parties, A, B, C and D fight an election using TR with 12 constituencies and 3 party seats and the votes cast are follows:

Constituency	Votes				Winner
	A	B	C	D	
1	**55**	20	15	10	A
2	**50**	15	20	15	A
3	**40**	10	_35_	15	A
4	**40**	15	25	20	A
5	**40**	15	25	20	A
6	**35**	25	30	10	A
7	20	**40**	30	10	B
8	20	**40**	30	10	B
9	25	**30**	25	20	B
10	25	**35**	15	_25_	B
11	30	10	**40**	20	C
12	_35_	10	**40**	15	C
Total votes	415	265	330	190	

In a FPTP election the result would have been:

Party	Votes	Share of votes	Seats	Share of seats
A	415	34.6%	6	50.0%
B	265	22.1%	4	33.3%
C	330	27.5%	2	16.7%
D	190	15.8%	0	0.0%

Here A is the party with most support and it wins in half of the constituencies in spite of having a little more than a third of the votes. Party B, although not having as many votes as C, wins two seats more than C, while D fails to win in any constituency.

With TR, the losing votes for each party (those shown in italics) are now counted. These are:

A	155
B	130
C	250
D	185
Total	720

With 720 votes cast for losing candidates and 3 party seats to allocate, the average per party seat is 240. However, only C had more than 240: it is given a party seat and its total reduced by 240 to 10. The two parties with the 'highest remainders' are now A and D and each is therefore given one of the remaining party seats.

The result now becomes:

Party	Share of votes	Constituency seats	Party seats	Total seats	Share of seats
A	34.6%	6	1	7	46.7%
B	22.1%	4	0	4	26.7%
C	27.5%	2	1	3	20.0%
D	15.8%	0	1	1	6.7%

Although not a proportional result, it is a much fairer one. Party A was a clear winner in terms of votes, but not such a clear winner as to get half of the seats. Even in the constituencies it did not win it, it averaged nearly 26 votes – sufficient for it to be awarded a party seat. Party B had fewer votes than C but, as can often happen with FPTP, it had more seats than C. With TR, C is compensated with a party seat, as is D which did not win in any constituencies but which had significant support.

The party seats would have been awarded to the parties' best losers – those underlined in the table of votes.

In this election, 40% of voters voted for a winning constituency candidate. If this had been a FPTP election, the other 60% of voters would have been unrepresented. With TR, however:

- 40% of voters voted for successful constituency candidates;
- 49.2% of voters voted for unsuccessful constituency candidates but their votes helped other candidates of their preferred party to win;

- Only 10.85 of voters did not contribute to the election of any candidate.

Thus only 10.8% of voters would have been without representation either by a constituency they had supported or by another member of party of the candidate they had supported.

TR – a simple solution

Aharon Nathan has therefore given us a simple way of overcoming some of the worst faults in FPTP. Like many simple but effective ideas, it leaves us wondering why no-one thought of it before. Although it is not a proportional system, and does not set out to be one, it will produce fairer results without any need to change the way people are accustomed to voting. It will drastically reduce the number of wasted votes and in doing so will give all electors an incentive to vote for the candidates of their preferred parties.

CHAPTER 4

Tailoring TR to taste

In the last chapter we described the essential features of TR. Like most other voting systems, however, it can be tailored to take account of what we want to achieve in elections. We now look at the choices to be made when introducing TR and the issues that lie behind them.

How many party seats and the case for proportionality

Party seats are allocated to parties according to the number of votes received by their losing candidates. The more party seats to be allocated, the more it will be possible for compensate parties for their support in constituencies in which they did not win and the better the opportunities for smaller parties to win seats (in our example, if there had been only 2 party seats to allocate then party D would have failed to get representation). From the voters' perspective, the more party seats the better the chance that their votes, if not cast for winners, will help their parties win more seats.

TR, however, seeks to augment rather than undermine the idea of an essentially single-member constituency system. Party seats are intended to give some compensation to voters whose candidates did not win, but not to the extent that almost as many losers as winners end up in parliament. While those elected in constituencies and those allocated party seats will have the exactly the same status in parliament, it is the intention of TR that the majority of MPs should represent constituencies and be responsible to the electorates of these constituencies. The number of party seats should therefore be much less than the number of constituencies.

There is a further argument, however, for having a small ratio of party to constituency seats, and that is proportionality. The more party seats there are, the more proportional the outcome is likely to be, but TR was designed, with the Israeli experience in mind, to avoid proportionality. For Britain, however, we must think about what level of proportionality we should seek to achieve.

Many electoral reformers have proportional representation – PR for short – as their main objective. In its pure form, PR means that a party's share of the seats is as near as possible to its share of the votes. That level of purity, however, is difficult to achieve – Israel is one of the few countries that gets close to it and, as we have noted, Israel's voting system has more problems than positive features. What most thoughtful reformers want is a move in the direction of proportionality. They want a move towards a system that will be fairer to parties (and therefore to voters) and will not produce the gross distortions of FPTP (remember Labour's win in 2005 with only 35% of the votes) – what is often termed 'broad proportionality'.

Proportionality, at least in moderation, is a good thing. We elect a parliament to debate issues and vote on them on our behalf. The decisions that parliament takes should generally reflect the views of the electors it represents and that will only happen if the make-up of parliament reflects strength and diversity of views within the electorate. Parliament, it can therefore be argued, should be society in miniature – if an opinion is held by, say, a third of the electors then it should be held by roughly a third of the politicians.

Proportionality also leads to a more diverse parliament. It gives smaller parties more chance of gaining seats and significant minorities more chance of having their views represented. In the 2010 general election UKIP received 919,546 votes but did not win any seats, but with pure proportionality it would have won 20. Whatever we think of UKIP, we have got to accept that its treatment at the hands of FPTP has been unfair. A parliament with a wider range of voices is likely to have fuller debates – it does not mean that smaller parties will often get their way, but it does ensure that more points will be considered.

Parliaments, however, have another function. They determine which party, or parties, will form the government. For a government to be effective, some argue, it needs to be able to put forward a programme with a reasonable expectation that it will be accepted, albeit with minor revisions, by the parliament. Sometimes governments will need to put forward proposals that do not command majority support in the country, for example when taxes must be increased or services cut. Unless the government has a majority of the votes in parliament, it will find it hard to implement its policies.

Proponents of FPTP argue that a main advantage of the system is that it has generally produced governments which are decisive because they are strong in the sense that they command a majority in parliament, even if they lack a majority in electoral support. PR, as we have seen in Israel, can lead to a highly fractured political system without any dominant party and with a plethora of minor ones. A government with a parliamentary majority can only be formed by deals between the parties that will form a coalition – hardly the best way making policy in a democracy – and any proposals for contentious legislation are likely to lead to defections from the coalition which could cause the downfall of the government. Making it too easy for small parties to win seats, it is claimed, can encourage people to vote for them rather than focussing their attention on to the major parties that will determine policy.

The arguments against proportionality are, however, overstated. There are countries across Europe, and indeed the world, that have fairly proportional voting systems but also strong government, and we certainly don't want a government that is 'strong' in the sense that it do whatever it wants on a minority mandate. Nevertheless, the arguments of PR's opponents have some validity and there is therefore a case for seeking a compromise between full proportionality and the disproportionality of FPTP.

However, if we want to move in the direction of proportionality, there is another factor we need to consider. In Britain's parliament there is very little appetite for PR – indeed, for most MPs the very idea is abhorrent. It is of course understandable that MPs have a liking for the system that gave them their seats, and no major party will react warmly to a proposal that would reduce their seats and consequently their influence. The Liberal Democrats and smaller parties have much to gain from PR and therefore support it enthusiastically (which is not to deny that for many it is an issue of principle, but it is easier to have principles when principle and self-interest converge), but there is only a small band of PR advocates in Labour (for most Labour politicians who support AV, it was as far as they were prepared to go), and there does not appear to be more than one Conservative MP that would countenance proportionality.

Thus, however strong the intellectual case for broad proportionality might be, any proposal for more than a modest step in its direction is doomed to failure. If our objective is to achieve change, then there is little point in advocating a change that is a non-starter – we need to approach our task considering not just what we think desirable, but what is politically possible.

These arguments have led to Aharon Nathan proposing for national parliaments a ratio of one party seat for every 4 constituencies, i.e. party seats would be 20% of the total. Although that appears a sensible compromise, in chapter 8 we will consider whether 1:5 might be a better option for UK general elections. For other levels of government different percentages can be used, and in chapter 9 we will examine how a 1:3 ratio could make local government much fairer.

National or regional allocation of party seats

A first issue to consider is whether party seats should be allocated nationally or on a regional basis. The arguments are as follows:

- If allocation is done across the whole country, there are many more votes and party seats to consider. For example, for the UK, with its 650 constituencies, we would have 162 party seats to allocate (assuming a ratio of 1:4), but if we work regionally, in all regions other than the South East (the largest), the number of party seats would be less than 20. The larger the number of seats to be allocated, the more chance small parties have of gaining representation. To win one of the 162 party seats, a party would need only 0.6% of the votes that did not win constituency seats – perhaps little more than 0.3% of the total votes cast, but in a region with, say, 15 party seats a party would need just over 6% of the losing votes to be sure of winning a party seat. A national allocation would therefore result in a more proportional outcome with many very small parties gaining representation.

- A question that must be asked, however, is whom MPs represent. For constituency MPs is it clear – they represent all their constituents no matter how they voted. Party MPs, however, are elected across the entire country or across a region, so who do they represent? Being representatives of a region is difficult – MEPs, who are elected regionally, face this task and are often perceived as being remote from ordinary voters - but to be elected nationally would mean that Party MPs may be representatives of those who voted for their party, but would not be linked to any geographic area and would be cut off from the casework that keeps MPs connected to the problems and concerns of ordinary electors.

Thus, although national allocation may be good for very small parties, for the UK with its 650 constituencies, it risks producing Party MPs without a clear geographic mandate. Moreover, the ease with which tiny minorities could gain representation might be considered a drawback. Regional representation could overcome this problem, allowing significant minorities to win seats and at the same time ensuring that all MPs are linked to, and accountable to, a geographic area. While Aharon Nathan has proposed national allocation for Israel with its 120 seats, for the UK, working on a regional basis may be preferable.

Allocating party seats

Party seats are awarded to parties based on votes for their losing candidates. This is done in a proportional way – if a party had a quarter of the losing votes, then it would be given a quarter of the party seats.

The mathematics, however, is rarely that simple - how many seats, for example, is a quarter of 6? There are several proportional methods to choose from, but the one advocated by Aharon Nathan in his original description of TR is the 'Largest Remainder Method'. Here is how it works:

1. the total number of losing votes is divided by the total number of party seats to give the average number of votes per party seat - those who study electoral systems call this the 'Hare quota';
2. each party is given a seat for each whole number of this quota of votes it has;
3. the remaining seats are then given to the parties with the highest remainders after their votes are divided by the quota.

Let's take an example. Suppose there are four parties (A – D) and five party seats to be filled, and the votes cast for losing candidates are as below:

Party	Votes	Stage 1 Divide by quota (20)	Stage 2 Seats for full quotas	Stage 3 Seats for highest remainders	Total seats
A	55	2.75	2	1	3
B	26	1.30	1	0	1
C	11	0.55	0	1	1
D	8	0.40	0	0	0

In total there are 100 votes, so the quota is 20. For full quotas, A gets two seats and B gets one, leaving two for the highest remainders. These go to A (with 0.75) and C (with 0.55).

There are other ways in which party seats could be allocated to parties, including the D'Hondt method which is already used in Britain for allocating seats in European Parliament elections and for regional seats for the Scottish Parliament and the Welsh and London assemblies. The D'Hondt method is not as generous to small parties as the Largest Remainder method – in the above example it would have given 4 seats to A but none to C – but the Sainte Laguë system, which is a variant of D'Hondt, would have given the same result as the Largest Remainder method. The choice of method therefore depends on where we want to strike the balance between helping small parties gain representation and making it possible for parties to win with very little support.

However, unless there are good reasons for doing otherwise, the Largest Remainder method seems appropriate. TR produces a fairer apportionment of seats amongst the larger parties but, not being a particularly proportional system, does not threaten their dominant positions. It does not give smaller parties anything like shares of the seats proportional to their shares of the votes, but it seems reasonable to opt for a method that is more likely to give them at least a voice in parliament.

We will return again to the choice of method for allocating party seats in chapter 8 when we consider how TR might be used in UK general elections.

If party seats are allocated over a large area (i.e. one in which a large number of party seats are to be allocated), a further consideration is whether there should be a threshold for gaining seats. For example, if in the 2010 general election party seats had been allocated nationally using a ratio of 1:5 (without any changes in the number of constituencies), there would have been 130 party seats. Without a threshold, to be assured of winning a seat a party would only need less than 0.8% of the losing constituency votes, and as these votes were only 53% of the total votes, parties could win seats with less than 0.4% of the vote, and perhaps much less if seats are won through a 'largest remainder'. Whether or not that would be a good thing, or whether a party should be required to pass, say, 1% of the total vote to gain representation, is a matter of judgement. Allocating seats regionally, however, overcomes this problem: in a region, for example, with 15 party seats the quota would be just over 5%, and although parties could win seats with less, those with fewer than around 3% of the votes would be unlikely to be successful.

Filling party seats

Once it has been determined how many party seats a party wins, these seats are then given to the party's 'best losers'. Best losers can be determined either by:

- The candidates with most votes
- The candidates with the highest percentages of the votes.

If all constituencies are more or less equal in size and have the same turnout, both approaches will produce the same winning candidates. But if they are not, there may a choice to be made. Consider the positions of two losing Labour candidates in the 2010 general election:

Constituency	Labour Votes	Percentage of vote
Caithness, Sutherland & Easter Ross	7,081	24.6%
Inverness, Nairn, Badenoch & Strathspey	10,407	22.1%

Which candidate did better? Caithness, Sutherland and Easter Ross is a small constituency in terms of the number of electors (and will remain so in the boundary changes proposed for the next general election), and Labour's 24.6% of the vote amounted to only 7,081. However, in Inverness, Nairn, Badenoch & Strathspey, a constituency with almost one and a half times as many electors, the Labour candidate did much better in terms of votes, but his vote share was lower. If we work on the basis of actual votes, then candidates in smaller constituencies will be disadvantaged, and therefore using percentages might seem fairer.

However, even when we have constituencies of similar size, the percentage of the vote a candidate wins will not just depend on how may voters he or she attracted, but on how many people voted for other candidates. Take two constituencies in the West Midlands:

Constituency	Turnout	Lib Dem Votes	Percentage of vote
Stoke-on-Trent Central	53.2%	7,039	21.70%
Warwick & Leamington	72.3%	8,977	18.35%

In a sense the Liberal Democrat in Warwick and Leamington did better by getting more people to vote for him, but as a result of the very high turnout (perhaps a consequence of the campaigns of his opponents), his percentage was lower than that of his colleague in Stoke-on-Trent Central.

In the great majority of cases both approaches will select the same candidates. Given the proposals to make constituencies nearly equal in size, the use of votes may be the best approach, and indeed that is what has been proposed by Aharon Nathan. It does make it harder for candidates in the very small number of Scottish constituencies which will remain much smaller after the boundary changes, but it seems the lesser problem.

Aharon Nathan has proposed that party leaders who do not win their constituency seats should be given a party seat (assuming their party wins one) before any other seats are filled by best losers. In Israel, where a change to TR would mean introducing constituencies for the first time with all the uncertainty that might entail, this appears sensible, at least as an interim measure. In the UK, however, where party leaders must face the electorate in their constituencies without any guarantee of success, and where voters can reject leaders who have lost popularity, giving this extra protection to party leaders may be unpopular and undesirable. A strict application of the best-loser procedure therefore seems best.

By-elections

What if an elected member dies or resigns while in office? If the member is a constituency member, a by-election would be held, just as happens at present.

If a party member were to resign, however, there would be no need for a by-election. The seat would be offered to whoever was the next best loser of the same party in the original election (or the next best loser prepared to take the seat as the circumstances of former candidates might have changed). In the unlikely event of no former candidates of the same party being prepared to take the seat, it would remain vacant until the next election.

This approach to filling casual vacancies is the same as is used in elections to the Scottish Parliament and Welsh and London assemblies – elections which involve constituency and regional candidates (see chapter 6).

CHAPTER 5

What differences would TR make?

How TR would change elections

With TR, elections would not look much different from our present FPTP system. Parties would select their candidates in just the same way, there would be a candidate from each of the major parties in every constituency, and there may be candidates from small parties and even independents. People would vote as they do at present, putting an 'X' against their preferred candidate and the votes would be counted in usual way. No-one could claim that TR is difficult – the only change from FPTP is in what happens after the votes have been counted and the constituency results declared.

However, people would vote knowing that their vote might matter, even if they sense that their chosen candidates are highly unlikely to win. They would therefore have much more incentive to go out to vote. Party members, where they know their candidate cannot win the constituency, would nevertheless have a reason for campaigning as their votes could help their party to win party seats – perhaps even for their own candidate: TR could therefore breathe a little more life into some local parties, many of which are fairly moribund.

Safe seats under FPTP would remain safe under TR. However, there is nothing wrong with a constituency returning a candidate of the same party election after election if there is a clear majority for that party in the constituency. What is wrong with safe seats is that they effectively disenfranchise supporters of parties that have next to no chance of winning, but TR overcomes that problem by using their votes in the allocation of party seats.

Tactical voting would remain possible – some may still vote for a candidate other than the one they really want in order to try to prevent someone they don't want from winning a constituency seat. But it would be less common as people would know that a sincere vote for their preferred candidate could help their party gain a party seat. As a result, with TR we might see an increase in support for parties such as the Greens whose supporters might, under FPTP, decide to vote for a potential winner rather than wasting their votes.

What TR would mean for parliament?

TR would produce fairer, slightly more proportional results, but not to the extent that it would be too difficult for parties to win an outright majority of seats should they have a significant lead over their opponents. Although it is possible for TR to produce a less proportional result than FPTP, this is very unlikely to happen (for example, while AV would have given Labour an even more exaggerated majority in the 1997 general election, TR would have slightly reduced Labour's lead).

Parties that do well under FPTP would also do well under TR. If a party won, say, 40% of the seats under FPTP, it is likely that they would win around 40% of the constituency seats with TR. If there were one party seat for every 5 constituencies, then that party would have 33%[8] of the total seats from the constituency contests alone and it would be very likely to win a good share of the party seats as well.

In chapter 8 (and appendices 1 and 2) we will look at how TR might have affected recent general elections in the UK: modelling of elections shows that the Conservatives and Labour would still have been the dominant parties, each winning a share of the seats higher than their share of the votes. The Liberal Democrats, however, who never get anything like their share of the seats in FPTP elections, would do much better under TR, although not to the extent of getting seat shares to match their vote shares. UKIP, and even the Green Party and the BNP could on occasions have won seats giving them a voice in parliament but not the ability to change the outcome of parliamentary votes – unless a vote was an exceptionally close one.

Thus while results with TR would be a bit fairer, TR would not change the general shape of a parliament and only when there is a very close result under FPTP would TR lead to a different government. When we take the UK parliament as an example and look at all elections since 1992, we find that, with the possible exception of 1992, the FPTP winners would have formed the government, although with less exaggerated majorities and, in the case of 2010, a slightly fairer balance of strength between the coalition partners.

That there would be a few MPs from smaller parties would ensure that more minority viewpoints are heard in debates, although the three major parties would still have won 92.7% of the seats (compared with 95.7% under FPTP). If the party seats

---

[8] I.e. 40% of 5/6ths of the total seats.

had been allocated on a national basis, then more small parties would have gained seats. If TR had been used, of course, some people might have voted differently: the Green Party's vote in general elections probably does not reflect that party's support as Green voters may vote tactically knowing that the Greens will not win in their constituency, but with TR there would be more case for voting Green in hope of gaining a party seat.

For some, that TR might on occasions enable the BNP to win seats will be a cause of concern. However, well over half a million people voted for the BNP and it cannot be right to seek a system that denies representation to a significant minority just because we abhor many of their views. If we perceive the BNP to be a threat to our democratic ideal of political equality for all citizens, irrespective of their ethnicity, we must not attempt to counter it by abandoning that ideal. We will defeat the ideas of the BNP by creating a fairer politics based on reason and respect – not by trying to manipulate the voting system to exclude them in a manner that would also exclude other small parties from our political debates.

Many who argue against proportional systems do so on the grounds that it increases the likelihood of hung parliaments, and consequently coalitions or minority governments. They need not worry too much about TR, however, because its small degree of proportionality would only increase the chances of a hung parliament very slightly. Indeed, to find an election in which TR might have led to a different outcome we need to go back to 1992. That year the Conservatives suffered a net loss of 41 seats but still managed a narrow majority – 336 MPs in a parliament of 651. With TR they would still have had a clear lead over Labour, but less than an overall majority. However, as a Labour-Liberal

Democrat coalition would not have had a majority, we would probably have had a Conservative, or Conservative-dominated, government (see appendix 2 for details).

However, that TR slightly tips the odds towards hung parliaments should not overly concern us. If no party has near a majority of the votes, why should we want to give just one party control of the Commons, allowing it to implement policies that were opposed by a majority of voters? Claims that coalitions are weak and do not reflect what people voted for don't wash. We want a government that is strong in the sense that it has a strong democratic mandate. Disraeli may have declared that "England doesn't like coalitions", but opinion polls suggest that most people would like to see parties working together in government to tackle the nation's problems. During the Great Depression of the early 1930s and when at war in 1939-45, Britain needed strong government and opted for coalitions, and more recently coalitions have worked well in Scotland and Wales. Throughout Europe most countries have coalition governments, and it would be hard to argue today that Germany's government is weak because it is a coalition. There can, of course, be good coalitions and bad coalitions, just as single-party governments can be good or bad: this is not the place to pass judgement on the coalition government formed in 2010, but the experience of the 2010 general election demonstrates that FPTP can also result in coalitions, and the trend from two-party to multi-party politics increases the chances of hung parliaments whether or not we change the voting system.

What TR would mean for representation

We have already noted the TR would make parliaments more representative, but how would representation change for the elector?

With FPTP, one MP is elected in each constituency and that MP is regarded as the representative of all electors in the constituency. This, however, is a bit of fiction. Certainly MPs 'represent' their constituents in the sense that they will handle personal issues brought to them by constituents, irrespective of the political views of the constituents. However, MPs cannot, and will not, represent the political views of all their constituents – that would be quite impossible. On European issues, for example, an MP who is a strong supporter of the EU cannot represent the views of a UKIP supporter, and those opposed to fox hunting cannot expect the support of a fox-hunting MP.

Whatever a constituent's view might be of their MP, that MP is the only person they can turn to when they need an MP's services (parliamentary protocol does not allow MPs to accept casework from another MP's constituents). Thus with FPTP many, if not most, supporters of a party can only approach an MP who belongs to another party. In many cases that can be hugely detrimental to the quality of representation. Someone, for example, with a problem over immigration status might get a rather unsympathetic response from an MP who takes a strong line in immigration control, while in another constituency someone with a similar problem might find their MP is willing to energetically fight their corner with the Home Office.

Those problems could be overcome with TR. Each constituency would be represented by a Constituency MP, but there would also be Party MPs representing people in a wider region of which the constituency is a part (or even the entire country depending on how party seats are allocated). As a result, most people would find they had a MP of their preferred party to whom they could turn. For example, following the 2010 general election, in only 307 of the 632 constituencies in Great Britain (excluding Northern Ireland) did Conservative voters have a Conservative MP under FPTP. With TR, however, in the other 325 constituencies Conservative voters would at least have had a Conservative MP in a party seat in their region. Similarly, all Labour[9] and Liberal Democrat supporters would have had either an MP of their party in their constituency or in a party seat in their region. In all Scottish and Welsh constituencies there would have been either an SNP or Plaid MP or a party seat MP to represent the interests of supporters of these parties.

If a constituent felt their local constituency MP was unlikely to be sympathetic, they could instead choose to approach a Party Member in their region. Their choices might be based on factors other than party affiliation – on some issues women might feel more comfortable approaching a woman MP, or a younger person or an older person, or someone of similar ethnicity.

Issues do, however, arise over the roles and responsibilities of party members (issues that TR has in common with the

---

[9] Here it has been assumed that party seats would be added to the 650 constituencies used in 2012. If the total size of the Commons were reduced to 600, it is possible, that with fewer party seats, Labour might not have won any party seats in the North East. Consequently in the few constituencies of the North East not won by Labour, Labour would have had neither a Constituency nor a Party MP.

Additional Member System (AMS) which we will consider in chapter 6). Aharon Nathan has proposed that Party MPs should represent supporters of their party in their region (assuming a regional allocation of party seats) and this may well be how things work in practice. However, in the UK our tradition is that politicians are elected as people and not just as agents of their parties, and it might therefore be more reasonable, at least in the British context, for Party MPs to be seen as being there to represent any who care to use their services (as we have noted, some might choose which MP to approach on other than party lines).

In the UK context, allocating party seats regionally might help to give Party MPs more defined areas of responsibility, and it would also ensure that Party MPs cover the whole country, giving all regions equal representation. With a regional remit, it would be possible for them to develop a better knowledge of the areas they represent and it would avoid the danger of many Party MPs basing themselves near Westminster. An elector in, say, the North West could either approach the Constituency MP or a NW Party MP (some flexibility would be desirable for smaller parties that might not have Party MPs in all regions).

Experience of the Scottish Parliament and Welsh Assembly, where AMS also produces regional members alongside constituency representatives, suggests that Constituency Members would deal with the majority of the casework. There have been frictions where a regional member has opened an office near to one of a constituency member, and it is reasonable to expect a Party Member to seek an office in the constituency in which they were a candidate (not only will that be the area they know best and in which they are best known, but they may also look to future elections in which they might again be a constituency candidates). However, although Constituency Members might feel uncomfortable at having rivals of a different party working on what they regard as their patch, from the voter's perspective, which is surely more important, having more than one member they can approach is an advantage. In Scotland protocols have been introduced whereby regional MSPs must inform constituency MSPs of casework they are handling in their constituencies – this avoids duplication of effort as constituents may want to approach more than one member – and the same practice could make sense with TR.

What about independents?

TR, with its innovation of party seats, is a party-based system. It assumes candidates are representatives of parties and that a vote for a candidate of a party means support for that party. But any voting system worthy of consideration should not disadvantage independent candidates. How then would independents fare under TR?

Under our present FPTP system, of course, wins for independents in general elections are rare events and generally only arise in very exceptional circumstances. In recent years we have seen only three – the Kidderminster Hospital candidate who won in 2001 and 2005 on campaign against the closure of a local hospital, the 'Independent Labour' candidate who won Blaenau Gwent in 2005 when the local Labour party rebelled against a women-only shortlist, and Martin Bell who defeated a Conservative in Tatton on an anti-sleaze campaign in 1997 (although he was not an independent in the strict sense as he was not opposed by Labour or the Liberal Democrats). In local government, however, it is much more common for strong local candidates, often with a record of service to their communities, to stand as independents and win.

As TR is an FPTP election with the addition of party seats, it would be no more difficult for an independent to win under TR as under FPTP – any independent able to win a seat under FPTP would win the same seat under TR. Moreover, FPTP is not a bad system for independents – they are generally people with strong support in their own areas but little support outside it, and proportional systems in which elections must be fought over larger areas can therefore disadvantage them (STV, however, which does not take account of parties, is a notable exception to this rule).

Independents can of course be regarded as single-candidate parties. If an independent failed to win a constituency seat but came close to doing so, it is possible the candidate could win a party seat.

In conclusion

I have argued that a change from FPTP to TR would not be radical, and it would certainly not be radical compared to a change to STV. This chapter has demonstrated that a change to TR would nevertheless result in significant differences:

- TR would make parliament more representative of how people voted. It would not produce proportional results, but it would avoid the gross distortions of FPTP and would give some smaller parties a chance of gaining seats. It might not lead to different governments, although where FPTP would give a party only a slender majority, it might result in a minority government or require the leading party to seek a coalition partner and, as has been argued, that would not be bad for democracy. TR would give some smaller parties a voice at Westminster, but only if an election were to produce a very close result could smaller parties change the outcome of parliamentary votes.

- TR would result in many more voters finding that their votes had contributed to the election of an MP, and consequently many more voters would feel they are represented in government. Only a small proportion of voters would find themselves without either a constituency MP of their choice or a party member of their preferred party in their region.

Even if these changes are not radical, they are certainly changes worth making, and ones that can be made without changing the way people vote and without diminishing the transparency of elections.

CHAPTER 6

TR v. the alternatives

When we come to choosing voting systems, there is no shortage of choices. In what circumstances, however, is TR the right choice? In this chapter we will look at how TR compares with other voting systems on offer.

Although the number of voting systems is almost unlimited, it is possible to divide them into three broad categories:

1. Systems that only use single-member constituencies (and as a consequence cannot guarantee any degree of proportionality);
2. Proportional (or broadly proportional) systems that use multi-member constituencies (or 'electoral districts'), i.e. constituencies each of which elect several members in any election;
3. Mixed systems which combine a FPTP election in single-member constituencies with a list election to compensate for the disproportionality of FPTP.

We will now look at these three categories, and their strength and weaknesses.

Single-member constituency systems

These systems, which of course include FPTP, cannot guarantee even broad proportionality. To achieve proportionality, more than one candidate must be elected at the same time in the same constituency. If only one candidate is elected, only that person's supporters – perhaps the largest minority rather than a majority - will have representation; with two candidates the next largest group of voters can get a representative; with three it is possible for candidates of three parties to win (unless one party is strong enough to win more than one seat); and so on. The more candidates to be elected, the more proportional the system can be.

If we are contemplating change to make elections fairer, we can therefore eliminate such systems from our discussion. All systems which are based exclusively on single-member constituencies are about as capable of FPTP of producing highly distorted results and parliaments that come nowhere near to reflecting the spread of views in the country. Not all are as bad as FPTP – some, like AV, do more to prevent so many votes being wasted and avoid the possibility, which exists with FPTP, of the most unpopular candidate being elected. The French use the double-ballot system where, if no candidate gets more than 50% of the votes the voters return for a second round to decide between the two leading candidates but, when election turnouts are already low, there would be little appetite in Britain for asking voters to take part in two elections rather than one. Then there are systems based on the Condorcet method which, for every pair of candidates, asks who would win, but if AV was considered too complicated during the 2011 referendum campaign, these systems are non-starters. Some advocate

Approval Voting in which voters can vote for as many candidates as they want, but who wins often depends as much on party tactics as voters' preferences. Comparing all single-member constituency systems, AV comes out on top,[10] but as AV has already been defeated in a referendum, we need to look for something different.

Multi-member constituency systems

Here we need to consider list systems and STV.

List systems

With list systems a number of candidates are elected in a multi-member constituency (generally referred to as a 'district'). In each district, parties are awarded a share of the seats more or less corresponding to their shares of the votes. If a party gains around a quarter of the votes it will get around a quarter of the seats. In Britain we already use a list system for electing our MEPs.

List systems can achieve good proportionality but, when a number of candidates are elected in each district, the relationship between elected members and their constituents is weak. England's South East region, for example, elects 10 MEPs for an area stretching from Banbury to Dover and there can be little sense of identification between members and those they represent. As we have noted in chapter 3, Israel is an even more extreme case: the entire country is regarded as a single district

---

[10] For a comparison of different single-member systems, see Ritchie and Gardini, *'Putting Paradoxes into Perspective: in Defence of AV'* in *'Electoral Systems: Paradoxes, Assumptions and Procedures'*, Felsenthal and Machover (eds), Springer 2012.

electing 120 members. Thus when constituency representation is considered as important, list systems should be avoided.

The list system we use for European Parliament elections suffers from another defect. People can only vote for parties and not for candidates – those elected are the candidates parties have put near the tops of their lists, but they are not necessarily the most popular with the voters. Finland overcomes this problem by allowing people to vote for the candidates they want (an 'open list'): votes for candidates are considered to be votes for their parties, and if a party wins, say, 3 seats, then these will be given to that party's three candidates who received most votes. Many other European countries go half way by allowing people to vote either for their parties or for particular candidates: while this might seem a reasonable approach, in practice it is flawed as who is elected is often determined by votes just for parties and the candidates may be defeated by others with fewer personal votes.

The Single Transferable Vote

STV deals with districts in a much more sophisticated way. People vote preferentially, i.e. rather than marking the ballot paper with a single cross, they rank the candidates (or as many of them as they wish to rank) by putting a '1' against their first choice, a '2' against their second and so on. They need not confine themselves to candidates of just one party – a voter might, for example, give a first preference to a Labour candidate, a second to another Labour candidates, but a third to a Green.

In each district the number of votes a candidate needs to get elected – the 'quota' - is calculated. The first choices of the voters are counted, and candidates with the quota or more are elected: if a candidate has more than the quota, their vote is reduced to the quota by passing their ballot papers to the candidates marked as the second choice, but with each of those ballot papers counting as only a fraction of a vote. If there are seats still to be filled after all votes have been transferred from successful candidates, the candidate with fewest votes is eliminated and their votes given the next names on the ballot papers. Transfers and eliminations continue until all the seats have been filled.

This all might seem rather complicated, but voters need not concern themselves with the mechanics of the count. The way people complete an STV ballot paper is exactly the same as the way they would have voted with AV.

STV has been described as 'the connoisseurs' choice', and with good reason. People vote for the candidates they want to represent them rather than just for parties and, assuming that most people choose their candidates by party affiliation, it will produce results broadly proportional to party support. If, however, they chose candidates by some other criterion, such as age, gender or ethnicity, then it would produce results proportional by that criterion. With STV very few votes are wasted as ballot papers will be passed from one candidate to another until they find one that has a chance of winning.

So, STV is great and wins over TR and other systems hands down? It's not quite so simple.

Like list systems, STV is opposed by politicians who insist on the 'unique link' with constituents that FPTP provides (although not to the same extent as in practice STV generally uses smaller districts – only of 3 or 4 members in the case of Scottish local government). The arguments for a unique link are, of course, nonsense. The same politicians who tell us that in all walks of life, including these days in public services, choice and competition are good, refuse to allow choice and competition when it comes to representation. In their constituencies (and they often talk of their constituencies as if they owned them) they have a monopolistic position – they alone can speak in parliament on what they perceive to be their constituents' interests, and constituents requiring the services of an MP must turn to them – whatever the constituents' view of the MP, they have no alternative.

The only argument for single-member constituencies (without any party seats or their equivalent) that might have any validity is that it may prevent buck-passing: an MP approached by a troublesome constituent may, it is argued, simply leave the matter for another MP to handle. The argument is weak however: not only do MPs ignore constituents at their peril, but it ignores the fact that at present if an MP decides (perhaps for understandable reasons) not to assist a constituent, that person has nowhere else to go.

The great majority, and perhaps all, MPs are prepared to undertake casework for their constituents, irrespective of whether the constituents support them in elections, and in that sense a single MP can represent everyone in a constituency. But a single MP cannot represent all constituents politically: the MP has only one vote in parliament, and it is impossible for them to represent divisions of opinion within their electorates. The more MPs there are representing a constituency, the more chance of different viewpoints being heard.

However, even if we dismiss the unique-link arguments, STV presents some small, but irritating, problems:

- Counting STV elections is complex. Although hand counts are perfectly possible, when Scotland introduced STV for its local elections in 2007, it decided to use vote-counting machines. One of the arguments that defeated AV in the 2011 referendum was that elections would be much more costly as vote-counting machines would be needed: for AV this was quite false, but in changing to STV the argument would have much more validity.

- Voting with STV would be just the same as voting with AV – voters mark candidates in their order of preference – and it is easy. Nevertheless, claims that change would make voting more difficult was another of the effective arguments used against AV.

- With ballot papers that list candidates in alphabetic order, where a party stands more than one candidate, the candidates near the top of the ballot paper have a very much better chance of election than those near the bottom. There are ways round this problem[11], but they add to the complexity and cost of the elections.

- Proponents of STV argue that it gets rid of safe seats but when districts are relatively small and parties decide to stand only one candidate, it is not always the case.

---

[11] In parts of Australia they use Robson's Rotation in which successive ballot papers issued have the candidates listed in a different order in a predetermined way that ensures no candidate has a positional advantage. In some local elections in New Zealand, the order of the candidates on the ballot paper is randomised at the point of printing: bar codes against candidates names allows electronic vote counting.

- Being a candidate-based rather than a party-based system, all candidates compete with each other, even if they belong to the same party. This problem can be overstated – candidates are likely to do better if they are seen to be working in harmony with party colleagues – but is nevertheless a source of opposition to the system.

In spite of these drawbacks, STV is a good system in that it offers proportionality (and only modest proportionality if small constituency sizes are used), it allows people to vote for candidates and not just parties and, because votes are transferable, it greatly reduces the number of wasted votes.

Mixed systems

Mixed Member Proportional systems (MMP)

As the name suggests, MMP systems are hybrids. They can achieve proportionality, or a degree of it, by combining a single-member constituency election with an election using a list system. People have two votes – one for the constituency election and the other for a party list. In allocating the list seats, account is taken of the number of constituency seats won by the parties to create as proportional a result as possible. The form of MMP used for Scottish Parliament, Welsh and London Assembly elections we call the Additional Member System (AMS).

Elected members all have the same status, irrespective of whether they have been elected from constituencies or regional lists (although, as we will discuss below, their perceived status might not be so equal).

Clearly TR has similarities with AMS. Both systems start with FPTP in single-member constituencies and then a smaller number of seats are added to produce a fairer, more proportional result. With TR, however, electors only need to cast one vote – the constituency vote. Another important difference is that, in allocating party seats under TR, no account is taken of how many constituencies a party has won. In this respect TR is closer to the 'Parallel' systems used by some countries. Parallel systems are similar to MMP, but the list votes are allocated quite independently of the constituency votes, allowing strong parties to take many of the list seats as well as their constituency seats.

Proponents of AMS argue that it is better than list systems or STV in that it retains single-member constituencies and the unique link between elected members and their constituents. That, however, is only partly true. In Scotland, for example, where AMS is used for the Scottish Parliament, 73 MSPs are constituency members, but the other 56 are more loosely attached to wider regions. Every elector has 8 MSPs and not just one – a constituency member and 7 regional members. No-one has voted for these regional members – only for their parties: consequently they owe their positions to their parties who placed them sufficiently high on their lists, and they do not have the same, personal, mandates of the constituency members. It is the constituency members who do most of the casework and who receive most publicity in their constituencies, and opinion polls have shown that most electors regard the constituency members as more important. The regional MSPs have been described as "second-class members".

With TR, there is of course a danger that party members might similarly be regarded as second-class. However, party members would gain their seats as a result of the votes they received in the constituencies they fought, thereby giving them greater legitimacy.

However, its creation of two separate categories of elected members is not AMS's only problem:

- In some regions party list votes may have no effect. Consider the Glasgow region in Scotland. In the first two Scottish Parliament elections (1999 and 2003) Labour won all 10 constituency seats and in 2007 it won 9 out of 10. As Labour had well over its fair share of seats from the constituencies alone, it was not entitled to any regional seats, in spite of the fact that it had more party votes than of its rivals. In these years there was little point in Labour supporters giving their party votes to Labour. Although the system sought to produce a fairer result overall, there were predictable cries of "unfair" from some Labour quarters. Having two votes may increase voter choice, but that does not mean that all voters know how to sensibly use them. The Glasgow case (above) is just one example: Labour voters with any understanding of the system and wanting to make their votes effective would have given their regional vote to a party other than Labour, but in the 1999, 2003 and 2007 elections around 40% of Glasgow's voters voted Labour. While it is not necessary for voters to understand the counting rules, it is important that they know how to effectively use their votes, but opinion polls have shown that many do not.
- There has been controversy over whether people should be allowed to stand both as constituency and list

candidates ('dual candidacy'). Small parties may want to field their strongest candidates in constituencies where they have a chance of winning but, recognising the dangers of them not doing so, also place the same candidates high on their regional lists. As a result, many who lose in constituencies win through the lists. While Scotland continues to allow this practice, it was banned in Wales when in one constituency 4 out of the 5 candidates won – one winning the constituency and another three being elected as regional candidates. Parties other than Labour were outraged, regarding the change, understandably, as a move by the Labour government at Westminster to make life more difficult for them. That such issues can arise with AMS is not to its advantage.

- A result of the Welsh ban on dual-candidacy was that in 2011 the then Conservative leader in Wales, Nick Bourne, was effectively defeated by his own party. He was a list candidate as the Conservatives, having been weak in Wales, tended to rely more on the lists for their seats. In 2011, however, the Conservatives did much better in Wales and by gaining a constituency seat in the leader's region, they were no longer entitled to a regional seat. He lost not because he did worse, but because his party did better. Paradoxes of this nature don't help in building confidence in the system.

None of these problems would arise with TR. With TR there is no need for the second, 'regional' vote and therefore no problems arise over how to use the second vote effectively. With TR all candidates are constituency candidates, so neither the issue of dual candidacy nor the 'Bourne paradox' could arise.

Nevertheless, AMS has the advantage of being a well tried and tested system, and it is not an option we can easily discard.

Hansard AMS: a near neighbour

There is a version of AMS, however, which comes very close to TR and which therefore deserves special attention. In 1976 the Hansard Society set up a commission to review the electoral system for the Commons and what it recommended was AMS but with two important differences from the systems used in Scotland, Wales and London:

- Instead of electors having two votes, one for the constituency candidate and the other for their preferred party, voters vote with only a single 'X' in the constituency contest, and the 'additional' regional seats are then awarded to parties to achieve broad proportionality as measured by all the constituency votes;
- Instead of parties having lists of candidates for the regional seats, these seats will be filled by the losing constituency candidates who received most votes (or the highest vote shares): thus if a party was entitled to, say, 3 regional seats, it would be that party's 3 losing candidates who came nearest to winning who would fill them.

The Hansard version of AMS is therefore very similar to TR: with both systems people vote as in a FPTP election; in each case regional/party seats are awarded to compensate for FPTP's disproportionality; and in both the regional/party seats are won by the parties' best constituency losers.

If broad proportionality is an objective, then Hansard AMS scores over TR, but if only a more modest correction of FPTP is wanted then TR is the system to choose. As with other forms of AMS, in regions in which, say, Labour is strong, with the Hansard system in constituencies which Labour did not win Labour votes would be redundant, and there would be many more constituencies where supporters of a major party may have neither a constituency nor a party list member.

The Alternative Vote Plus (AV+)

Before leaving AMS we should mention AV+, the system recommended by the Jenkins Commission in 1998. AV+ is a form of AMS, but instead of using FPTP for the constituency elections it proposed to use AV. As AV is a better system than FPTP, AV+ is better than AMS. However, it suffers from all of the same problems as AMS, and as AV was defeated in a referendum, partly on the grounds that it was perceived as complicated, winning a referendum on AV+ would be a hard task.

So when should we choose TR?

All voting systems have their good points and their defects, and the table on pages 86 and 87 summarises their pros and cons.

There is not such a thing as a perfect voting system and, indeed, there is not even any agreement on what 'perfect' would mean in this context. For some, a voting system should be proportional, but others regard too much proportionality as a drawback, believing it can create problems in forming stable governments; for others a strong link between representatives and the constituents who elected them is the most important thing, even if having it is at the   expense of fairness; and there

	Representative outcomes		Voting
	How proportionality is achieved	*Degree of proportionality*	*Method of voting*
Lists	Use of multi-member districts	Good (if districts sufficiently large)	One vote for a party (or for a candidate if open of semi-open lists are used)
STV	Use of multi-member districts	Good/Fair (if districts sufficiently large)	Preference voting
AMS	Regional Members added to Constituency Members taking account of overall proportionality	Good/fair (depending on ratio of constituency / regional seats and size of regions)	Two votes: a constituency vote and a regional party list vote.
Hansard AMS	Regional Members added to Constituency members taking account of overall proportionality	Good/fair (depending on ratio of constituency / regional seats and size of regions)	One vote for a constituency candidate
AV+	Regional Members added to Constituency members taking account of overall proportionality	Fair (depending on ratio of constituency / regional seats and size of regions	Two votes: a constituency vote (by AV) and a regional party list vote.
TR	Party Members added to Constituency Members with PMs proportional to losing constituency votes	Fairer than FPTP but not truly proportional.	One vote for a constituency candidate

	Voting (continued)	Accountability		Counting
	Voter choice	*Candidate or party based*	*Constituency link*	*Complexity / ease of count*
Lists	Poor – cannot choose candidate (although some choice if open or semi-open lists used)	Party	Weak	Relatively easy
STV	Excellent	Candidate	Quite strong	More complex
AMS	Quite good: a vote for a constituency candidate and one for a party (not necessarily that of the constituency candidate)	Mixed	Strong for constituency members, weak for regional members	Not difficult, but two stages required
Hans-ard AMS	Limited – as FPTP	Candidate, although number of regional seats determined on a party basis	As AMS, but regional members determined by personal rather than party votes	Not difficult, but two stages required
AV+	Good – as AMS but with preference voting for the constituency candidate	Mixed	As AMS, but stronger for constituency members because of use of AV	Not difficult, but more so than AMS and TR because of use of AV
TR	Limited – as FPTP	Candidate, although number of regional seats determined on a party basis	Not difficult, but two stages required	Not difficult, but two stages required

are different opinions on the importance of all representatives being elected on the basis of votes they have received personally, rather than as a result of votes for their party in general.

In choosing which voting system to use for any election, the first step must therefore be to decide what we want to achieve. Only when we have done that can we think about which system would best serve the purpose. The system we think most suitable for one set of elections might be very different from the system we choose for another - with voting systems it is therefore horses for courses. The question we must now ask is in what circumstances is TR the front runner? TR could, of course, be used in any election and, as we can vary the ratio of constituency to party members and the regions over which party members are allocated, it can be adapted to the requirements of particular elections. This does not mean that TR will be the right choice in every case, so let's look at where TR would be not just appropriate, but also the best choice.

TR has been devised to:

- tackling situations in which a measure of fairness is needed, but not necessarily a high degree of proportionality;
- making most votes contribute to the result, and thereby going some way to ensuring that voting is important, even in constituencies where the outcome of the election can be considered a foregone conclusion;
- ensuring the accountability of most members to their electors through a majority of members being elected in single-member constituencies, and through making party

seats dependent on votes cast for individuals and not just their parties;

- ensuring that voting is easy.

When that is the job we want done, TR is a possible answer, and possibly the best one.

Fixing our broken democracy

Part 3: TR for the UK

CHAPTER 7

When should TR be used in the UK?

Until 1997, all British elections used FPTP (although Northern Ireland already had STV for local elections), but since then the UK has become a laboratory for the study of voting systems. Whatever we think of the Labour government elected that year, it must be given credit for changing the look of British democracy. It introduced a regional list system for European Parliament elections, AMS for devolved government in Scotland, Wales and London (all with different ratios of constituency to regional seats), STV for the Northern Ireland Assembly and the Supplementary Vote (SV) for mayoral elections, and the new Scottish Parliament later introduced STV for Scottish local government. In electoral terms, the only, and the major, fault of that government was its failure to deliver on its manifesto pledge to offer a referendum on how we elect our MPs.

In each case, the choice of system was preceded by debate on what was wanted from the different elections, and different criteria led to different choices. For general elections, which lead to the formation of governments, there has been resistance to proportionality and the idea that electors in each constituency should be represented by a 'unique' MP has prevented moves from FPTP, despite its disadvantages. At the other end of the scale, MEPs are not expected, at least to the same extent, to attend to the problems of individual constituents so the link between constituents and representatives is regarded as of the same importance, but European Parliament rules and the nature of the Parliament (a more representative body that does not need to form an executive) means that much greater priority must be given to party proportionality – hence the use of a list system. For the Scottish Parliament and the Welsh and London Assemblies, a compromise has been struck between these two extremes – with AMS a majority of members are elected in single-member constituencies but with regional members to give a degree of proportionality which is considered important. The choices that have been made may not have been the right ones, but the UK experience demonstrates how different perceptions of what an election should achieve have led to different solutions.

In choosing these voting systems, however, TR was not on the menu of options. What we now must ask is whether for any of these elections TR should have been considered, and indeed chosen. In the previous chapter we noted that TR would have been a good choice when there was a need for:

- greater fairness but not necessarily a high degree of proportionality;

- the accountability of elected members to geographic constituencies;
- a system that gives everyone an incentive to vote by minimising the number of wasted votes;
- a system that makes voting easy and is transparent.

If that's what TR can do, for which elections should it be used?

General elections

Most of this book is about how we elect our national parliament. The need to resolve the problems that FPTP creates in our general elections, described in chapter 2, has been the main reason for writing it.

General elections are clearly the most important elections we hold in the UK. They determine not just which candidates will become MPs, but also what sort of government we will have and who will be Prime Minister. It is the government, subject to the support of the Commons, that decides on the big questions of economic policy, public services, foreign policy and defence matters. Although some powers have been devolved, particularly to Scotland, Wales and Northern Ireland, it is the government that sets the overall budgets and the frameworks in which devolved bodies, as well as local government, must operate. That makes it more important than for any other elections that we get the voting system right, yet changing the voting system for the Commons has proved to be more difficult than for any other level of government. Part of the problem is that so much is at stake in a general election, and part is that the decision on

93

the voting system is in the hands to the people – the MPs – who will be most affected by change.

The problems of FPTP in general elections are such that even many of the most resolute opponents of reform concede that FPTP is far from satisfactory, but there is no consensus on what should be done about it. Most electoral reformers, and particularly the smaller parties that are squeezed out of power by FPTP, want a change to a broadly proportional system, but proportionality is something the larger parties are, perhaps understandably, set against. This has created an impasse with neither side willing to give ground (perhaps for fear of jeopardising their negotiating positions). It is therefore possible that progress will only be made when there is a compromise proposal that gives reformers something of what they want while allaying the fears of at least some of reform's opponents.

TR could be that proposal. It does not offer reformers proportionality, but it does offer more fairness without threatening the positions of the major parties. We have argued that broad proportionality is a good thing, but we must also accept the strength of the opposition to it. The issue here is not which side is right, but what sort of change is politically possible, and politics is often about finding acceptable compromises. There will always be some opposition to change, and even the slight move towards proportionality that TR would make can expect resistance, but it would be difficult to argue there is anything unreasonable about TR.

Similarly, we have dismissed the idea that single-member constituencies are either desirable or necessary, but the reality is that a large majority of MPs will not countenance anything else. TR recognises this situation by ensuring that single-member constituencies remain the basis of elections.

TR would not get rid of safe seats, but it would ensure that votes for losing candidates in safe seats are not just wasted. Although it would not go as far as some proportional systems in making all votes of equal value irrespective of where they are cast, it would go a long way towards reducing the wastage of votes under FPTP and giving everyone more incentive to vote.

The case for using TR for general elections is therefore a strong one.

Local government

Scotland and Northern Ireland use STV for their local government elections. It is a decent system and there is no compelling reason for proposing that they change to something different.

Local government in England and Wales, however, is quite another matter. FPTP produces such distorted outcomes that even general election results look fair by comparison. In the 2005 local elections in London, in 6 of the 32 boroughs the party with most votes did not win most seats. In Cardiff in 2008, the Liberal Democrats won more than twice as many seats as its nearest rival in spite of having been third in terms of votes. What is more common than 'wrong winners', however, is the parties with most votes winning exaggerated majorities: in the 2009 county elections in Kent the Conservatives won over 88% of the seats on just 46.6% of the votes – on par with Labour winning 89.9% of the seats in Glasgow in 2003 (before the introduction of STV) on 47.6% of the votes.

The use by many local authorities of multi-member FPTP[12] (in which several candidates are elected together in multi-member ward) can make the distortions of FPTP worse as a party with just a few more votes than any rival can win all seats in the ward. Sketty ward in Swansea elects 5 councillors together: in 2008 the Liberal Democrats received 40.8% of the votes[13] but won all seats.

The case for changing the voting system for local elections in England and Wales is therefore a very strong one. Not only do all the arguments we have made against the use of FPTP for general elections apply, but the case against change is weaker: even with FPTP there are many hung councils with 'joint administrations' so the argument that we should keep FPTP to avoid coalitions does not have the same force and, as many councillors are already elected in multi-member wards, it is hard for opponents of reform to argue that multi-member wards are a bad thing. Nevertheless, opposition to the introduction of a proportional system is strong – if it

---

[12] Political scientists often refer to multi-member FPTP as the Multiple Non-Transferable Vote (MNTV) system.
[13] Calculating a party's electoral support is a problem when not all parties field a full slate of candidates. Here we have followed the convention of assuming the highest vote for any of a party's candidates to be the measure of the party's support.

were not, FPTP would probably have been abandoned years ago.

In Wales there has at least been a debate on the issue. STV was recommended by a commission[14] set up by the Welsh Assembly in 2001, and in the party negotiations that followed the 2007 election there was nearly a deal that would have delivered STV. However, as Labour won half of the Assembly seats in 2011, the prospects for STV disappeared – at least for some time to come.

If England and Wales are not prepared to follow the example of Scotland and Northern Ireland, then TR can come to the rescue. Just as with parliamentary elections, TR would produce fairer results, avoiding 'electoral deserts' (areas where a party has significant support but no, or very few, seats) and giving smaller parties better chances of getting a voice on councils (and in local government there are areas where even the Conservatives and Labour must be regarded as small parties). Many more voters would find their votes 'counted' – even if their preferred candidates were not successful, their votes could help win party seats for their party.

Other UK elections

We have argued for the use of TR for general elections and local elections in England and Wales – the only UK elections that use FPTP. With elections for other tiers of government, the case for broad proportionality has been accepted and

---

[14] The 'Commission on Local Government and Electoral Arrangements in Wales'

while TR could be used, it may not be the most appropriate choice of system. This is not because of any defect in TR – it is simply because the job to be done is a different one.

European Parliament elections

The criteria for choosing a voting system for these elections are quite different. Proportionality is not just desirable but there is an EU agreement that all member states should elect their representatives on a proportional basis. Unfortunately Britain uses about the worst proportional system it could have chosen for European Parliament elections and there is a strong case for changing to something better, but could TR be an answer? TR could be made more proportional by increasing the ratio of party:constituency seats, but even with one party seat for every two constituency seats would not produce an acceptable level of proportionality.

Scottish Parliament and the Welsh, Northern Ireland and London assemblies

Broad proportionality was one of the criteria used in choosing the AMS system for electing the Scottish parliament and the assemblies for Wales and London. AMS, as we noted in chapter 6, is a far from perfect system, but it has made the devolved bodies much more representative of the people of Scotland, Wales and London. There is a strong case for changing their voting systems to STV, which is used for the Northern Ireland Assembly, but losing their degree of proportionality by changing to TR would be unwise.

The Welsh Assembly is perhaps, however, a case that should be kept on the TR agenda. Labour is by far the strongest party in Wales, although it has never managed to pass 50% of the seats in the Assembly. Within Labour there are many who would like to abandon AMS to avoid the need to get another party's support to form a majority, but such a move away from AMS would be a retrograde step. If those opposed to AMS were to get their way, however, TR would be a much better alternative than FPTP.

Proposed elections for the Lords

The reform of the House of Lords has been on the political agenda for more than a century, but it was only following the election of the Labour government in 1997 that discussions started in earnest. Labour quickly acted to get rid of the anachronism of hereditary members – other than 92, elected by hereditary peers themselves, who were retained as a concession while the nature and composition of the second chamber was debated. After 13 years in office, however, Labour still had not resolved the matter. Commissions were established and long debates held in parliament, but things got stuck in the arguments not just over whether the Lords should be fully elected or partly elected but over what the Lords are there for. Following the 2010 general election, however, all parties seemed to be signed up to at least a majority of Lords (or whatever the members of a revised second chamber might be called) being elected, and the new coalition government promised to produce proposals for elections "on the basis of proportional representation". The debate, however, continues, and there remains a danger that progress will be thwarted by failure to reach agreement on the way forwards.

That the Lords should be elected by a proportional system makes sense. Unlike the Commons, its members are not engaged in case work and they are not required to represent particular geographic interests, so there is no reason for seeking a constituency-based system (although there is concern that Lords should not just be people who have worked and made their reputations in the South East). The main role of the Lords is to scrutinise and revise government legislation: they do not form an executive so arguments about the need for clear majorities and strong government do not apply. It is unlikely that a second chamber in which the party of government had a clear majority would be an effective check on government action, and a chamber in which an opposition party had a majority and therefore the ability to block all government proposals could make effective government extremely difficult. Proportional representation therefore seems to be the answer.

The Commons and the Lords should therefore be two very different bodies: the Commons, which is made up of constituency representatives and which forms the government, should be elected by a system such as TR that is fair, but not necessarily fully proportional, and is constituency-based, while the Lords needs a more proportional system.

We cannot, however, simply write off TR as system unsuitable for the Lords. There are still voices in the debate calling for elections by FPTP, and if it appeared that the case for proportionality was not going to be won, then TR would be a much better alternative.

Even if the government were to accept the case for proportionality but were to propose that it be achieved through a 'closed' list system in which voters could only vote for parties, then there might be an argument for TR. Although most Lords are affiliated to one party or another, the scrutiny role of the chamber makes it important that its members are of independent minds and not just people who will unquestioningly follow their party whip. That is more likely to be achieved through a system in which members are elected on the basis of votes they receive as individuals and not just on the basis of votes for their parties. If open or semi-open lists or STV were unlikely to win support in parliament, then there might be a case for advocating the sacrifice of some proportionality in order to get a system, such as TR, in which electors can vote for candidates on the basis of their personal merits. Although TR, even with a ratio of one party seat for every two constituency seats, would not provide the proportionality that would be desirable for Lords elections, it is a system that should be held in reserve in case the current debate leads to a wholly unsatisfactory proposal.

In conclusion

In chapter 6 we concluded that choosing a voting system was a matter of horses for courses. Having looked at the courses, it appears that the TR horse is the favourite when it comes to:

- General elections (the Grand National of UK elections), and
- Local elections in England and Wales (a very important Derby).

It does not mean that TR is not a runner when it comes to other elections, but it is with these elections, which use FPTP but need something much better, that TR offers clear advantages. In the next two chapters we will look in more detail at how TR might be used for general and local elections and the benefits it could provide.

CHAPTER 8

TR and general elections

Putting TR into practice

Now that we have described the features of TR and concluded that it could be a suitable system for electing our parliament, in this chapter we look in more detail at how TR might be applied to general elections.

The first thing that must be said is that, from the voter's perspective, introducing TR would not make any noticeable change – people would cast their votes in exactly the same way as they do with FPTP. People would not even need to know that the system has changed (although we hope they will!) as they would just be asked to do what they have done in the past – put a cross against their preferred candidate. Change to AV or STV and voters need to be introduced to voting with numbers, and with AMS the significance of the two votes would need to be explained, in each case with extensive and costly educational campaigns (and not just for the first elections with a new system – surveys found that in the Scottish Parliament's second AMS election in 2003 understanding of the system was lower than in the first). For the voter, TR is by contrast simplicity itself.

However, in introducing TR there are a number of things we need to consider:

* what should be the ratio of Party seats to Constituency seats;
* how many seats there should be in total; and
* whether Party seats should be allocated across the whole country or on a regional basis:
* what method should be used for allocating party seats.

The ratio and number of seats

The only major change that TR would require would be in the redrawing of constituency boundaries. TR adds party seats to constituency seats, and if the size of the Commons is not to be increased, then the number of constituencies must be reduced.

The number of party seats, however, need only be quite a small proportion of total seats. With TR for general elections, we are not proposing the wholesale abandonment of FPTP – instead we only want to introduce party seats as a correction factor to avoid excessively unfair results and to ensure that the overall result takes account of more of the votes cast. The proportion of party seats should not therefore be more than 20%, i.e. not more than one party seat for every four constituencies (the ratio originally proposed by Aharon Nathan).

Let's consider how TR might affect the size of the Commons. The Conservatives won the 2010 general election (in the sense that they were the largest party) on a manifesto in which they proposed reducing the number of MPs by 10%, i.e. from 650 to 585, although in the parliamentary debates that followed a reduction only to 600 was agreed. If we were to introduce TR on the basis of these 600 constituencies and then add 150 party seats, we would have a parliament of 750 MPs. Whether or not that would be desirable, there is next to no chance of such an increase being politically acceptable. So what are the options?

1. If the number of constituencies were reduced to 500, a ratio of 1:4 would add 125 party seats giving a total of 625 – more than 600 but still a reduction from the 650 on which the 2010 election was fought (and with all previous elections there have been around 650 seats).

2. A reduction to 500 constituencies with a ratio of 1:5 would lessen the effect of TR, but not significantly so, and would result in the 600 seats now proposed for the Commons;

3. With a ratio of 1:5, we could have 542 constituencies and 108 party seats giving 650 in total – the same as in 2010;

4. To achieve a Commons of 600 seats with a ratio of 1:4 would require having only 480 constituencies with 120 party seats.

These options are summarised in the table below:

Option	Constituencies	Party seats	Total	Ratio
1	500	125	625	1:4
2	500	100	600	1:5
3	550	110	660	1:5
4	480	120	600	1:4

There are, of course, many other options we could consider, such as 542 + 108 or even 550 + 100, but the above four are enough to illustrate the nature of the choice to be made.

What is clear is that the number of constituencies must be reduced in introducing TR if the number of MPs is not to be increased. Redrawing constituency boundaries is of course quite possible for the Boundary Commission to do, but any proposal for major boundary changes would strike fear into the hearts of all MPs, leaving them all asking themselves how changes would affect their chances of re-election, and even of re-selection should their constituencies effectively disappear.

That does not mean, however, that getting the Commons to consider TR is a non-starter. Far from it. Any change in the voting system is likely to come about when a major party which supported it in opposition finds itself in government. If, in the circumstances we have following the 2010 general election, Labour were to back TR and in a subsequent election win power, or the major share of power, then it would find itself in government with a manifesto commitment to change, and a move to a fairer system would of course have the support of the Liberal Democrats and smaller parties. Moreover, having opposed the reduction from 650 to 600 MPs, Labour might not be averse to something along the lines of option 3 which restores the Commons to its former size but with only a slight additional reduction in the number of constituencies. (We will return to how the case for TR can be won politically in chapter 10.)

Thus while a 1:4 ratio of party to constituency seats might be desirable, a 1:5 ratio may make the introduction of TR easier to achieve. In appendix 1 (Part B) we will examine how the different ratios would have affected recent election outcomes.

National or regional allocation

Then there is the question of whether party seats should be allocated nationally or regionally. In chapter 4 it was noted that regional allocation would ensure regions have equal representation rather than some regions having more than their share of candidates elected to party seats. It would also avoid having MPs without any geographic base and would therefore make it clearer whom Party MPs represent and to which MPs, other than their Constituency MPs, electors should take their concerns.

Regional allocation would also be less proportional, making it more difficult for fringe parties to win seats. Whether we regard this as being good or bad, the major parties, whose support for any change must be won, would prefer regional allocation for this reason alone. If regions are sufficiently large, however, TR will still offer opportunities for minor parties with significant support.

The most obvious choice of regions would be those used for European Parliament elections (which, until 2010, were regions with devolved administrative powers). While they are not ideal in that they vary in size, from 18 constituencies in Northern Ireland to 82 in the South East Region, they have the advantage that they are already recognised and used for other elections.

Elsewhere,[15] however, allocation on a county basis has been suggested. This would have the advantage of tying party members more closely to geographic areas. Using the European Parliamentary regions would result in party members representing, for example, the whole of Scotland or an area that extends from Banbury to Southampton and Dover. Such large areas are difficult enough for MEPs whose work is more to do with regional issues and European legislation, but how an MP could 'represent' and accept casework from anywhere in Scotland in another matter. Allocating on a county basis would follow the recommendations of the Jenkins Commission which proposed AV+ with roughly the same number of 'additional seats' as party seats under TR. However, if TR were to be introduced with a ratio of one party seat for every 5 constituencies, allocating by counties has a drawback. A typical county has at present around 7 – 8 constituencies, and as a result each constituency would elect only 1, or at most 2, party members, giving very little opportunity for smaller or under-represented parties.

---

[15] Baston and Ritchie, 'Don't Take No for an Answer: The 2011 Referendum and the Future of Electoral Reform', Biteback Publications, 2011.

An alternative approach would be to subdivide larger regions into two, or even three, sub-regions. It would be desirable for sub-regions to have at least 30 constituencies, and undesirable for them to have less than 25.[16] Although some regions would be divided for the allocation of party seats and others would not, it does not mean that some are more favourably treated than others – in each allocation area the ratio of party to constituency seats would be the same. However, while the use of sub-regions has merits, it would not in every case enhance the geographic links of Party MPs: while Party MPs in the London region for north of the Thames and south of the Thames might make sense, a Party MP for the north and east of Scotland is not necessarily a great advantage over having Party MPs for all of Scotland. Moreover, dividing regions into sub-regions of more or less equal size would result in allocation areas which cut across county boundaries, leaving party members representing areas which are difficult to define.

When we come to look at how TR might have affected recent elections (below) we will assume allocation by region, but also in places refer to how outcomes might have been affected by a sub-regional allocation (sub-regional allocation of party seats is also considered in more detail in Appendix I).

---

[16] See appendix 1 for the basis for proposing sub-regions of this size.

Allocating party seats

In chapter 4 we described the Largest Remainder method which should be regarded as TR's default option for the allocation of party seats.

The D'Hondt method, however, also requires consideration, if only because it is already in use for European Parliament elections and elections for devolved government in Scotland, Wales and London. With this method, devised by the Belgian mathematician Victor D'Hondt in 1887, the first party seat is given to the party with most votes, and then that party's vote is divided by 2. The second seat is then given to the party that now has the greatest number of votes. After each seat is allocated, the votes for the parties are divided by one more than the number of seats they have already received before the next allocation is made. In this way it seeks to equalise, as far as is possible, the ratio of votes : (seats + 1) for all parties. Although it produces reasonably proportional results, it tends to be more advantageous to the larger parties, while it is possible that small parties might gain a seat using the Largest Remainder approach but not with D'Hondt.

The Sainte Laguë method is a variant of D'Hondt which gives smaller parties more chance of gaining seats. When a party is allocated a seat, its total vote is divided by twice the number of seats it has gained plus one: while with D'Hondt a party's vote is successively divided by 1,2,3, ... after the award of successive seats, with Sainte Laguë it is divided by 1,3,5, ... This means, for example, that when a party has been awarded a seat, it will not get another while there is another party with a least a third of its votes. Although the Sainte Laguë method is not used for elections in the UK, it is used for deciding how many European Parliament seats there should be in each region.

In order to see how the choice of method might affect results, suppose that the 2010 general election had used TR with a ratio of one party seat to every 5 constituency seats, with party seats allocated regionally, and with the same constituencies as in the actual election.[17]

	Constit seats	Party seats			Total seats		
		LR*	SL*	D'H*	LR	SL	D'H
Con	307	31	30	31	338	337	338
Lab	258	29	29	33	287	287	291
Lib Dem	57	45	49	53	102	106	110
UKIP	0	10	9	5	10	9	5
BNP	0	6	6	1	6	6	1
Greens	1	2	0	0	3	1	1
SNP	6	4	4	4	10	10	10
Plaid Cymru	3	1	1	1	4	4	4
Total	632	128	128	128	760	760	760

* LR – Largest Remainder; SL – Sainte Laguë; D'H – D'Hondt

The choice of method does not therefore greatly affect the distribution of political power amongst the three main parties, although the Liberal Democrats in particular do

---

[17] Although, as we have noted, the introduction of TR would probably require the redrawing of boundaries to reduce the number of constituencies, this assumption has been made to allow us simulate TR using actual votes cast.

better with D'Hondt. The Sainte Laguë method gives results similar to those from the Largest Remainder method, although it would deny two seats to the Greens. D'Hondt, however, greatly reduces the number of seats for the smaller parties (other than SNP and Plaid which, of course, are major parties in the regions they contest).

These figures point to the merits of the Largest Remainder method[18], with Saint Laguë a possible runner-up. With a 1:5 ratio of party:constituency seats and party seats allocated regionally, it gives representation to small but significant parties, but not to what might be regarded as fringe parties.

An issue which arises in any discussion of fairer voting systems is whether it is right to choose a system that benefits the BNP. If our aim is a better democracy, however, we must respect the ways in which people have cast their votes and the voting system should not be designed to benefit or disadvantage any particular party, no matter how much we detest them. The BNP did, after all, receive more than half a million votes – about twice as many as the Greens and even more than the SNP – and it would be a wrong to design a voting system to deny representation to any party with such support. The policies of the BNP need to be defeated by political debate – not by subterfuge. There may be a case for considering D'Hondt because it is a method of allocation that is already in use in UK elections,

---

[18] Although the Least Remainders method can suffer from the 'Alabama Paradox' whereby an increase in the number of seats to be allocated can reduce the number of seats a party wins, occurrences of this paradox ar likely to be exceedingly rare.

but no case for adopting it to keep out people whose ideas we abhor.

How might TR have changed recent election outcomes

If TR had been used in recent general elections, what difference would it have made? It is not a question we can answer with any precision for two reasons:

1. With any attempt to model an election using a different voting system, we cannot be certain that people would have voted in the same way. In FPTP elections, some voters might have voted tactically (possibly as many as 10% according to some research) in constituencies where they felt their preferred candidates had little chance. For example, in a Conservative-Liberal Democrat marginal, a Labour voter might have voted Liberal Democrat in hope of keeping the Conservative out rather than wasting a vote on Labour. With TR, however, votes for losing candidates are not wasted: the same Labour voter might decide to vote for the Labour candidate to help Labour win a party seat.
2. Introducing TR without significantly increasing the size of the Commons would require boundary changes, and how that would affect constituency results would depend on the detail of the changes the Boundary Commission would make.

Modelling the 2010 election using TR on the basis of existing constituencies

We can nevertheless get a fairly good idea of how FPTP and TR results would compare by calculating how many party seats the parties would have won if the TR election had used the same constituencies are the FPTP election (as we have done in the above comparison of the effects of different allocation methods).

Let's start by looking at London as an example. The results for London in 2010 were:

	Votes	Seats
Con	1,174,588	28
Lab	1,245,627	38
LD	751,603	7
UKIP	59,452	0
Green	54,316	0
BNP	52,095	0
Respect	17,368	0
Other	46,349	0
Total	3,401,378	73

We now look at the votes that were cast for losing candidates.

These were;

	1	2	3	4	5
	Votes for losing candidates	Votes for losers / quota	Party seats on full quotas	Party seats on largest remainders	Total party seats
Con	526,917	4.56	4	1	5
Lab	397,240	3.44	3	0	3
LD	579,145	5.01	5	0	5
UKIP	59,452	0.51	0	1	1
Green	54,316	0.47	0	1	1
BNP	17,368	0.15	0	0	0
Respect	52,095	0.45	0	0	0
Other	46,349	0.40	0	0	0
Total	1,732,882		12	3	15
Quota	*115,525*				

With 73 constituencies and a ratio of one party seat for every 5 constituencies, there would be 15 party seats in all (rounding to the nearest whole number of seats). Dividing the total votes for losing candidates by 15 gives a quota of 115,525. We then divide the losing votes for each party by the quota – this gives us column 2. In column 3 we give a party seat for every full quota – a total of 12 leaving three seats still to be allocated. In column 4 these seats are given to the parties with the largest remainders.

Adding party seats to constituency seats would have given the following results:

	Votes	Constituency Seats	Party seats	Total seats
Con	1,174,588	28	5	33
Lab	1,245,627	38	3	41
LD	751,603	7	5	12
UKIP	59,452	0	1	1
Green	54,316	0	1	1
BNP	52,095	0	0	0
Respect	17,368	0	0	0
Other	46,349	0	0	0
Total	3,401,378	73	15	88

This outcome would have been far from proportional, but it is a bit fairer as can be seen if we look at the figures in percentage terms:

	Percent of Votes	Percent of seats	
		FPTP	TR
Con	34.5	38.4	37.5
Lab	36.5	52.1	46.6
LD	22.1	9.6	13.6
UKIP	1.7	0.0	1.1
Green	1.6	0.0	1.1
BNP	1.5	0.0	0.0
Respect	0.5	0.0	0.0
Other	1.3	0.0	0.0

With FPTP, Labour won a majority of the seats in London with only 36.5% of the votes: with TR it would not quite have achieved a majority, which is a more reasonable outcome.

TR does not give the Liberal Democrats their proportional share of the seats but it gives them a better reward for their 22.1% of the votes. UKIP and the Greens gain a seat with TR, and the largest party not to win a seat – the BNP – had only 1.5% of the votes.

Repeating this exercise for all regions we can see what the national result in 2010 might have been with TR:

	FPTP seats	TR seats	Votes	FPTP seats	TR seats
Con	307	338	36.1%	47.2%	43.2%
Lab	258	287	29.0%	39.7%	36.7%
LD	57	102	23.0%	8.8%	13.0%
Greens	1	3	1.0%	0.2%	0.4%
SNP	6	10	1.7%	0.9%	1.3%
PC	3	4	0.6%	0.5%	0.5%
UKIP	0	10	3.1%	0.0%	1.3%
BNP	0	6	1.9%	0.0%	0.8%
Other	0	0	1.3%	0.0%	0.0%
NI	18	22	2.3%	2.8%	2.8%
TOTAL	650	782	100.0%	100.0%	100.0%

(Note that although a ratio of one party seat for every constituency would lead to 130 party seats and a total of 780 seats, rounding to the nearest whole number of party seats in each region gives a total of 782.)

These results would probably have led to the same coalition government, and with the same sort of majority (in percentage terms), as emerged in 2010. However, the Liberal Democrats would have had a much stronger voice in government. Labour and the Liberal Democrats together would have fallen short of a majority by only 3 seats.

Such an election would have given the great majority of voters representation by an MP of their preferred party, either through a constituency member or through a party member (or members) in their region. Looking at Great Britain (i.e. excluding Northern Ireland), the table below shows that all Conservative, Labour and Liberal Democrat voters would have had some form of representation.

| | FPTP | | | | TR |
	Constit MP	No MP	Constit MP	Party MP only	No MP
Conservative	307	325	307	325	0
Labour	258	374	258	374	0
Lib Democrat	57	575	57	575	0
UKIP	0	632	0	544	88
BNP	0	632	0	321	311
Green	1	631	1	156	475

In Scotland and in Wales, all SNP and Plaid voters would have had either a constituency MP or a party MP to represent them.

If larger regions had been divided into sub-regions of at least 25 constituencies (excluding Northern Ireland where there are only 18 constituencies), the Conservatives would have had three seats less, the position of Labour would have been unchanged and the Liberal Democrats and SNP would each have had an extra seat. This would have given Labour and the Liberal Democrats a combined total of exactly half of the votes, perhaps making a coalition between them more attractive but only marginally so. As sub-regions would reduce the number of party seats in each allocation, it would have been harder for small parties to win seats: although UKIP would have gained an extra 3 seats, the Liberal Democrats and SNP one each, while the BNP would only have won 3 and the Greens would have been left with their single constituency win.[19]

Regional details of these results are given in Appendix 1 (Part A).

Modelling the 2010 election with TR on 500 constituencies and 100 party seats

Here there is an extra element of uncertainty as we cannot be sure what the constituency results would have been on the changed boundaries. The best assumption we can make is that all parties would have been affected in the same way (although we know that in practice there would be winners and losers).

We will also assume that people would have voted in the same way as they voted in the actual election, and that for each party the totals of votes for their winning and for their losing candidates would have been the same. Clearly they would not have been, but it is the most reasonable approximation to make.

Using these assumptions, here is how a TR election in May 2010 might have looked:

---

[19] While rounding in regions led to 132 party seats, with sub-regions it gave a total of 130.

	1 FPTP actual	2 FPTP modelled	3 Party seats	4 Total seats
Conservative	307	236	23	259
Labour	258	198	23	221
Lib Democrat	57	44	37	81
UKIP	0	0	7	7
BNP	0	0	2	2
Green	1	1	0	1
SNP	6	5	3	8
Plaid	3	2	1	3
N Ireland parties	18	14	3	17
	650	500	99	599

Column '1' is the actual number of seats won in 2010. Column '2' has been calculated by multiplying the number of seats won by 500/650 and rounding. The total number of party seats is not exactly 100 because of rounding to whole numbers of party seats in the regions and, in columns '5' and '6', sub-regions.

With fewer party seats, the opportunities for small parties are not so great, and if party seats were allocated on a sub-regional basis then UKIP would be the only extra party that would have gained representation. However, none of the parties that failed to win a seat received more than 2% of the national vote.

In this case, whether party seats are allocated regionally or in sub-regions, Labour and the Liberal Democrats would together have had just over half of the seats and an alternative Labour-Liberal Democrat coalition would have been more feasible. However, given the approximations we have needed to make, quite apart from political considerations, whether TR on this basis might have produced a different government is hard to predict.

Modelling previous general elections

Applying the same approach to previous general elections – i.e. reducing the number of constituencies to 500 and adding around 100 party seats, allocating in regions – gives the following results (details can be found in Appendix 2)

2005 General Election

Labour won a majority of 66 seats in spite of having received only 35% of the votes. Consequently the Electoral Reform Society described it as "the worst election ever". Commenting shortly after the election, the late Robin Cook spoke of how outraged Labour would have been if the Conservatives had 'stolen' the election in a similar fashion. In the days following the election the Independent newspaper ran a campaign for electoral reform, but the then Lord Falconer, the then Lord Chancellor, drily remarked that he "saw no groundswell of support" for reform and government got on with business as usual. The Conservatives blamed unequal constituency sizes for their treatment by FPTP: while this was a contributory factor, it was a relatively minor one – the problem lay in the nature of FPTP.

TR would not have prevented a very distorted election outcome, but modelling suggests it would have left Labour just a slither short of a majority - 49.8% of the seats, which is far too close for us to say what the outcome might have been with any certainty. With more seats than the Conservatives and Liberal Democrats combined, Labour, even with less than half the seats, may have decided to form a minority government, but probably with another general election well before 2010, or they may have invited the Liberal Democrats to join them in a coalition, which might have produced much faster progress towards electoral reform.

2001 General Election

Labour had a hugely exaggerated majority, winning 62.7% of the seats with just 40.7% of the votes.

With TR, Labour would still have had a comfortable majority (about 55% of the seats and slightly more than twice as many as the Conservatives).

1997 General Election

This was a very significant election for British politics. It ended 18 years of Conservative government and brought in Blair's 'New Labour' government. Although a Labour win had been predicted, few Labour supporters expected the scale of their victory – a majority of 179 seats. However, although the election was regarded as a Labour landslide, Labour's 43.3% of the vote was only 1.4% higher than what the Conservatives received in their narrow win in 1992.

The election also saw gains for the Liberal Democrats; although their share of the vote dropped, by winning seats from the Conservatives they more than doubled their share of the seats to 7%.

TR would have given Labour a clear victory – around 56% of the seats but not the excessive majority (over 63% of the seats) they gained under FPTP. The Referendum Party, formed and funded by Sir James Goldsmith, which received 811,849 votes, would have won about 5 seats.

A criticism made of AV during the 2011 referendum campaign was that in 1997 AV would have given Labour an even greater majority. Not so with TR. The results under different systems might have looked like this:

		1997 share of seats	
	FPTP	AV[20]	TR
Cons	25.0	15.6	27.3
Lab	63.3	67.4	56.2
Lib Dem	7.0	12.6	10.7
Other	4.5	4.4	5.8

While AV would have produced a less proportional result, TR would have improved proportionality and the Conservatives, with 30.7% of the votes, would not have been so unfairly treated.

---

[20] Here we have taken the average of two estimates given in the House of Commons Library paper on 'AV and Electoral Reform' of June 2011.

1992 General Election

The Conservatives' win was a big disappointment for Labour which had approached the election with high hopes. On election day, however, the Conservatives had a clear lead with 41.9% of the votes to Labour's 34.4%, and a 21 seat majority.

Things would have been different with TR. The Conservatives would have fallen short of a clear majority, but would have had roughly the same number of seats as Labour and the Liberal Democrats combined (TR would have more than doubled the Liberal Democrats' share of the seats). It is likely that the Conservatives would have formed a minority government, but it would probably have been a short-lived one.

Summary

This is one of the longest chapters in this book, but as a principle recommendation of the book is that TR should be considered for general elections in the UK, is it also one of the most important. Let's summarise what we have concluded:

- If the size of the Commons is reduced to 600 members, TR might best be introduced with 500 constituencies and about 100 party seats. If it were politically feasible to restore the Commons to 650 or more members, however, 550 constituencies and 110 party seats (or 542 and 108) might reduce the impact of further boundary changes.

- The regional allocation of party seats would give party members geographic responsibilities and would ensure that all areas of the country are equally represented. The present regions used for European Parliament elections, although suffering from size differences, appear to be the obvious choice for regions.
- Party seats should be allocated using the Largest Remainder method as this increases the chances of small parties gaining representation.
- Looking at all general elections since 1992, it is unlikely that TR would have led to different governments, although:
  - in 2010 the Liberal Democrats would have had a much stronger voice in the coalition that was formed and, although a Labour-Liberal Democrat coalition would not have been likely it would have been more possible than with FPTP;
  - in 2005 Labour might have found itself very slightly short of a majority and it is possible that it may have felt it necessary to reach an agreement, even if short of a coalition, with the Liberal Democrats;
  - in 1992 the Conservatives would have failed to gain a majority, but as a Labour-Liberal Democrat coalition would not have done better, the outcome might have been a short-lived minority Conservative government.

Fixing our broken democracy

CHAPTER 9

TR for local government in England and Wales

Chapter 7 noted that TR could produce fairer local government elections in England and Wales. While Scotland and Northern Ireland use STV, other parts of the UK continue to use FPTP and resistance to any move towards proportionality has met stubborn resistance (although the debate on reform continues in Wales and the case for change was almost won in 2007). TR could make English and Welsh councils more representative of their voters without the more radical change that STV would entail. This chapter therefore focuses on England and Wales.

If we were to introduce TR for local government elections we would need to consider the same issues as we looked at for general elections:

* what should be the ratio of Party seats to Constituency seats (which we will call 'ward seats' to fit with local government terminology);
* how many seats there should be in total in a local authority area; and
* whether Party seats should be allocated across each local authority area or in subdistricts;

*   what method should be used for allocating party seats.

TR, as we have noted, could make local government elections a bit fairer but without going as far as proportionality, but it seems reasonable that for local government we should go further towards proportionality than the 1:5 ratio for constituency:party seats that we have recommended for general elections. We therefore propose a ratio of 1:2, i.e. for every two ward seats there should be a party seat (and, as we will demonstrate, this ratio allows the introduction of TR in many local authorities without the need for boundary changes).

However, as with the Commons, any proposal that would significantly increase the number of councillors in any local authority could expect to meet stiff resistance. We therefore need to find a way of introducing TR without increasing, or without increasing significantly, the size of existing councils.

Here we come up against a complication in that not all councils conduct their elections in the same way. Local government in England and Wales has a mix of ward sizes – some wards elect only one member while others elect two or three, and in Wales there are even 4- and 5-member wards. Many councils have 'all-out' elections in which all seats are contested every fourth year, while others have elections 'in thirds' in which only a third of the seats are elected in three years out of every four (in areas which have both district and county elections, county seats are elected in the years when there are no district elections). Let's look at each in turn.

Councils of 3-member wards with all-out elections

All of the London boroughs fall into this category. Here there is a very easy solution: each existing 3-member ward becomes a 2-member ward with the same boundaries, and the third seat becomes a party seat. With 2-member wards the principles of TR can be applied just as easily as with single-member wards.

Take, for example, the Coombe Hill ward in the London Borough of Kingston. The votes cast in the 2010 elections were:

	Candidate		
	1	2	3
Conservative	2455	2354	2304
Labour	521	495	458
Liberal Democrat	1314	1194	1019
Green	391		
Christian People's Alliance	82	77	68

Here the Conservatives won all three seats (with FPTP it is very often the case that in 3-member wards the same party will win all three seats).

If the election had been conducted using TR with each ward electing just two members, each of the parties would have fielded only two candidates. The votes then might have been (taking the top two candidates of each party):

	Candidate		Winning	Losing
	1	2	votes	votes
Conservative	2455	2354	4809	
Labour	521	495		1016
Liberal Democrat	1314	1194		2508
Green	391			391
Christian People's Alliance	82	77		159

(In a TR election there would of course have been a greater incentive for the Greens to field two candidates.)

Here the Conservatives win both ward seats, but the total losing votes of the other parties would be used to determine the allocation of party seats.

If the ward seats were split between two parties, the same principles would apply. On the same basis, the outcome under TR in Canbury ward in Kingston might have been:

	Candidate		Winning	Losing
	1	2	votes	votes
Conservative	2333	2283	2333	2283
Labour	711	678		1389
Liberal Democrat	2469	1927	2469	1927
Green	899			899

In this case the Conservatives and the Liberal Democrats win one ward seat each, but the votes of the losing Conservative and Liberal Democrat candidates are using in allocating party seats.

Thus TR works just as well in multi-member wards as in single-member wards and by making 3-member wards into 2-member wards, TR can be introduced without change in boundaries or the size of the council.

Councils of 3-member wards with elections in thirds

Many English councils, including the metropolitan areas outside London, are of 3-member wards in which only one seat is elected at each election.

The most obvious thing to do here is to change from elections in thirds to all-out elections. There is no evidence that elections in thirds produce better local government than all-out elections. They are, however, more expensive, both for local government and for local parties. For parties, whether a 3-member ward is electing one or three candidates, the same number or leaflets need to be delivered and the same number of doors knocked on, and fighting election campaigns each year is a much bigger drain on party resources. Although some argue that elections in thirds keep councils on their toes as in three years out of every four at least a part of the council must face the electorate, annual elections mean that administrations can be less stable, it is more difficult for them to take difficult but necessary decisions without fear of loss in seats, and parties must constantly be in election mode.

With this change from elections in thirds to all-out elections, local government becomes much cheaper but just as effective, and TR can be easily introduced, as above, but electing just two members in each of the existing wards.

Councils with a mix of ward sizes

The number of councils that fall into this category is declining as the Local Government Boundary Commission for England has tended to seek 3-member wards when major boundary changes have been needed. However, where there is still a mix of ward sizes, boundary changes would be needed. There are two options:

1. Make a change to wards which would elect 3 members if FPTP were used, but make each ward a 2-member ward and introduce TR as above;
2. Change to single-member wards, but with only the number of wards needed to elect two thirds of the seats (for example, a council of 60 councillors would have 40 single-member wards and the remaining 20 councillors would be elected in party seats): TR can then be introduced in the same way as described for general elections.

Either of these approaches would be perfectly satisfactory, although if TR is to be used (and even if FPTP were to be used), there is no real reason for opting for wards that elect more than one member. Indeed, in many rural areas single-member wards may be much more meaningful: for example, a village might prefer to have its own councillor, whatever that councillor's political affiliation, rather than to share 3 councillors with a wider group of villages. The only thing that would need to be avoided with TR is a mix of ward sizes in an all-out election as that would give voters in larger wards more voting power when allocating party seats (a voter in a 3-member ward might have 3 losing votes while a voter in a single-member ward would only have one).

Allocating party seats

Whether party seats should be allocated by pooling votes for losing candidates over the whole of a local authority area or over subdistricts is a matter that could be decided on a local authority basis. With small councils allocation over the whole area might be considered quite satisfactory and, by allocating more seats together, it would give better opportunities for candidates of smaller parties (for example, local parties campaigning for particular local interests) to win seats. However, the nature of local government suggests that all councillors should represent people in particular areas rather than parties as many of the issues councils need to consider are not ones of national politics or political ideology. Dividing the local authority into subdistricts should therefore be the preferred option unless there are reasons for doing otherwise. Subdistricts, however, should be large enough to offer a reasonable number of party seats – subdistricts of 12 councillors (8 from wards and 4 party members) might be a sensible minimum.

The choice of method for allocating party seats is much the same as the choice for general elections, although it might be argued that in local government there is a stronger case for allowing parties that represent small minorities to gain seats of councils: this points to the largest remainder method.

Some examples

Kingston

We have already looked at two wards in Kingston Borough, but how would TR have affected the 2010 election in Kingston? This council is a Conservative-Liberal Democrat battleground: it has 16 three-member wards, giving a total of 48 councillors and, as with all London boroughs, all seats are elected every fourth year. In 2010 the Liberal Democrats won 27 seats to the Conservatives' 21: no other parties won any seats.

With TR each ward would have elected just two, rather than three, ward members – 32 in all – and the other 16 councillors would have been elected to party seats.

Rather than having party members elected over the whole borough, we have assumed that the borough would be divided into three subdistricts –

- Kingston Town (6 wards)
- Coombe and Malden (5 wards)
- Kingston South (5 wards)

With any simulation of how an election might have looked under a different voting system some caution is needed as we cannot be sure that people would have voted the same way. In Kingston, for example, where the contest is between the Conservatives and the Liberal Democrats, it is possible that Labour and Green supporters voted tactically for Liberal Democrat candidates but, with TR in which other parties could win party seats, more might have been inclined to cast 'sincere' votes for the candidates they really wanted. However, for the purposes of this illustration, we will assume that in any ward the votes for a party's two candidates would have been the highest two votes received by any of the party's candidates in the FPTP election.

With TR, as we have already noted, smaller parties would be more likely to ensure they have a full slate of candidates to increase their chances of winning party seats. We have therefore assumed that any party that contested at least half of the wards in a subdistrict would have had two candidates in each ward. Where there was not a candidate in the actual election, we have assumed that the extra candidates under TR would have received 90% of the lowest vote of any of its candidates in a subdistrict (we have used 90% because, if a party did not field a candidate in a ward it was probably because they assumed their support was weak).

With TR using these assumptions, the election result would have looked like this:

	FPTP				TR			
	Kingston Town	Coombe & Malden	Kingston South	TOTAL	Kingston Town	Coombe & Malden	Kingston South	TOTAL
Con	6	12	3	21	4	9	4	17
Lab	0	0	0	0	1	1	1	3
Lib Dem	12	3	12	27	12	4	9	25
Green	0	0	0	0	1	1	1	3

The Conservatives and the Liberal Democrats would still have been the dominant parties, and the Liberal Democrats would still have had a majority of seats (although a very narrow one). Labour and the Greens, however, would each have won 3 seats. The result would have been far from proportional (the Liberal Democrats had not much more than 40% of the votes), but it would have added extra voices to council debates.

Camden

While Labour was an also-ran in the 2010 elections in Kingston, in the London Borough of Camden it won more than half of the seats with almost exactly a third of the votes. If the election had been run using TR, Labour would still have been very much the largest party, but without a majority and with other parties winning fairer shares of the seats.

As with Kingston, Camden can be divided into three subdistricts – North, South and West – each of 6 wards. With FPTP each ward elected 3 councillors, but with TR each would elect 2 and 6 party seats would be allocated in each subdistrict. Using the same assumptions as before, the result under TR would have been:

	FPTP				TR			
	North	South	West	TOTAL	North	South	West	TOTAL
Con	2	0	9	11	3	2	7	12
Lab	10	17	3	30	8	11	4	23
Lib Dem	5	1	6	12	5	4	6	15
Green	1	0	0	1	2	1	1	4

Birmingham

Birmingham City Council also uses 3-member wards, but here elections are held in thirds. As a result, in each ward in every election there is only one candidate of each party and voters mark the ballot paper only with a single cross. Here we need to make an additional assumption to make a comparison of possible FPTP and TR results: if in the 2010 election a Labour candidate received, say, 1000 votes, we will assume that all three Labour candidates in an all-out election would each receive 1000 votes, and with TR each of the two Labour candidates would get 1000. Clearly this would not happen in practice – some candidates are more popular than others of the same party, and in some wards candidates of different parties would be elected – but it should be a good enough assumption for illustrative purposes.

Birmingham has 40 wards, each with 3 councillors. Rather than having Party councillors covering the whole of the city, Birmingham could be divided into 4 subdistricts, each of 10 wards:

- North
- West and Central
- South West
- South East.

In 2010 Labour won 36.9% of the votes but won 20 seats - half of the 40 seats that were being contested. Using the above assumption, in an all-out election they would have won 60 of the 120 seats on the council. With TR, however, they would have won only 51, which is 42.5% of the total. The results would have been as follows:

	FPTP (modelled)					TR				
	North	West & Central	South West	South East	TOT	North	West & Central	South West	South East	TOT
Con	15		18		33	12	3	3	14	32
Lab	15	27	9	9	60	13	19	9	10	51
Lib Dem	0	3	18	3	24	3	7	13	4	27
Green	0	0	0	0	0	1	1	1	1	4
Respect	0	0	0	3	3	0	0	0	3	3
BNP	0	0	0	0	0	1	0	1	1	3

This would have been a much fairer outcome as can be seen if we compare the shares of the seats with the shares of the votes:

	Votes (%)	Seats (%)	
		FPTP	TR
Cons	27.5	27.5	26.7
Labour	36.9	50.0	42.5
Lib Dem	24.1	20.0	22.5
Green	2.6	0	3.3
Respect	2.2	2.5	2.5
BNP	4.8	0	2.5

Although the BNP received nearly twice as many votes as the Greens, they would have won one seat fewer: this is because the BNP fielded only two candidates in the West and Central subdistrict. As with general elections, some will ask why we should want to change to a system that gives seats to the BNP. The answer is 'democracy'. With a proportional system, the BNP would have won 5 seats instead of the 3 they would have won in this illustration and it would be wrong to choose a voting system to deny representation to a party just because we find it distasteful. A better voting system, and the better politics that it can encourage, is the way to combat extremists.

Why TR would be better for voters

Having more representative councils must be in voters' interests. Where a council is dominated by a single party there is a danger the scrutiny of executive decisions will be weaker. A more representative council will generally mean a stronger opposition and often the presence of small parties that can contribute alternative ideas: as a result, there may be more debate and better decision-making.

However, there is another way that TR can improve representation. People are more likely to feel they are being listened to if they have a councillor who shares their views and can speak on their behalf. If their ward councillors are not of their party, which is the fate of around half of voters in most FPTP elections, they may feel unrepresented on many issues. With TR, however, even if their ward councillors are not of the party they supported, it is quite likely that there will be another councillor in a party seat in their area to whom they can turn. (Councillors will usually deal with casework for constituents whatever their political inclinations, but that is not the same as representing their views.)

Take Camden as an example. Of the 18 wards, in only 4 do Conservative supporters have a councillor of their party, in only 11 is there a Labour councillor and there are only 7 wards where Liberal Democrats have a councillor. With TR, in all 18 wards supporters of any of the three major parties will have either a ward member or a party-seat member representing them. After the 2010 elections, there is only one ward with a Green councillor, but with TR Green supporters in the other 17 wards would have had a party-seat councillor representing their views.

Part 4: The way ahead

CHAPTER 10

TR: a winnable reform

TR has arrived on the scene as what appears to be an answer to an increasingly pressing problem. Our FPTP system for electing our MPs was never a good one, but when Britain had an essentially two-party system of politics it produced broadly acceptable results. Generally it gave an advantage to the winning party and, although in 1951 and February 1974[21] the party with most votes did not win, in those years the two main parties were neck-to-neck in popular support and that the 'wrong' party won was not seen as a major problem.

We no longer have, however, a two-party system. Until 1970, the combined vote of Labour and Conservatives hardly fell below 90%, and together they won around 98% of the seats. With changes in society and the weakening of traditional party loyalties, more people are prepared to give their votes to other parties: what became the Liberal Democrats grew in strength as did the nationalist parties in Scotland and Wales. But the advances these parties made in

---

[21] In 1974 there was a second general election in October.

terms of popular support were not reflected in election outcomes: in the 2010 general election, although the Conservatives and Labour together received only 65% of the votes, they won 87% of the seats. Our voting system is simply not capable of reflecting the present-day plurality of our politics.

We cannot simply dismiss such distorted results as being consequences of the rules of the game. Elections are about who runs the country and who take decisions on our behalf. Our nation's democratic credentials are undermined while we stick with a voting system that does not produce governments that have the legitimacy that comes from wide popular support. It surely was not right that the 2005 – 2010 Labour government could impose its will on the Commons when only 35% of voters supported it in the 2005 election, and although a majority of voters supported one or other of the coalition partners in 2010, the coalition is dominated by the Conservatives who only received 36% of the votes. With only 57 MPs to the Conservatives' 307, the Liberal Democrats are only a minor partner, but this does not reflect that, in terms of votes, the Conservatives were only stronger by a margin of 3:2. With a different voting system that better reflected popular support the dynamics of the coalition, and therefore its policies, might have been quite different, and we might even have had a different coalition.

The case for changing the voting system is therefore overwhelming, but it is the voting system itself that makes change difficult. There will not be change until our politicians decide to allow it, or allow us to vote for it in a referendum.

But the parties who benefit from FPTP have little incentive to change the system that gives them so much advantage, and individual politicians have an understandable tendency to support the system which gave them their election victories.

Electoral reformers (this author included) have spent years arguing the merits of proportionality, the benefits of preference voting, the need to make more votes 'count' and the case for changes sufficiently radical to change the shape of politics. Against the weight of the political establishment, however, their efforts have had little impact. Although they won the chance to make a very modest change to AV, in the 2011 referendum they suffered a miserable defeat. In the post-referendum gloom, many fear that electoral reform, at least for the Commons, is off the agenda for a generation, if not a lifetime.

The issue is of such importance, however, that we must not simply assume that nothing can be done. What is needed is a new project, and one capable of commanding broad enough political support to achieve success. But there is no point in electoral reformers continuing to press for STV, or for whatever their favourite system might be, if it cannot win the support of politicians at Westminster. It is of course argued that how people choose their MPs should be for the voters and not the politicians to decide, and that is how it should be in an ideal world, but until there is a Commons majority that either supports reform, or allows an opportunity for reform, nothing is going to change. Any project that does not take account of the political realities is doomed to failure. It must be recognised that electoral reform will not be driven by the intellectual arguments around which system is best. Instead, electoral reform is a political process, and politics is about finding the compromises that will work.

That is why TR offers reformers a viable project. It is a good system in that it would give fairer results and reduce the number of wasted votes, but this book does not argue that it is perfect. It does not offer the more sophisticated choice of STV; it will not fully satisfy those for whom proportionality is the goal; it will only produce results than are fairer rather than fair; and it does not attempt to address the problems some see in safe seats. Its modesty, however, is its strength. There are some for whom any change will be threatening, but as TR would not unduly undermine the dominance of the major parties and as it would retain the single-member constituencies that so many MPs regard as important, it is unlikely to frighten too many horses. Moreover, unlike some other systems, none can reasonable oppose it on the grounds that it is too complicated for voters.

In TR Aharon Nathan has therefore given us a potential winner. The simple idea that parties should be given some compensation for their votes that do not lead to the election of an MP is so grounded in common sense that it should leave us wondering why no-one thought of it before.

Winning at Westminster

This book has been mainly about how we elect our MPs, but of course TR could also be used for any other tier of government. With European Parliament elections, elections that may be held for our second chamber (the 'Lords') and elections for devolved assembles, different criteria may lead us to different choices. If proportionality is major objective and if a constituency-based system is not considered necessary, then a list system or STV, or even AMS, might be the answer, but where we want to negotiate a step beyond FPTP in the face of concerns over change of any nature, then the case for TR is compelling.

A compelling case, however, is not enough to bring about political change. The howls of protest that greeted Labour's 2005 election victory with only 35% of the votes made very little impact on the views of MPs, most of whom were perfectly satisfied with the system that had given them their jobs. It did not have any impact on the Conservatives: although they had every reason to denounce a system that had given such benefits to their main opponents, they no doubt saw FPTP as the system most likely to make them 'elected dictators' when it came to their turn to govern.

In 2010 it was the Liberal Democrats who, as usual, were big losers under FPTP – they approached the election with high hopes but when it came to polling day the two-horse nature of FPTP re-asserted itself, leaving them as only a minor party in the governing coalition. FPTP's treatment of the Liberal Democrats (and of the minor national parties) was never of great concern to the two major parties, but at a time when they were regarded by Labour as having sold principles for power and by the Conservatives as being an unwelcome guest in government, there was little sympathy for them. A compelling case for change from FPTP could have been made, but the intellectual arguments for changing the voting system were never on their own going to determine the outcome of the AV referendum – politicians may have talked about what was good or bad for democracy, but the decisive issues were about party politics and many took pleasure in the outcome not just because AV was lost, but because it put the Liberal Democrats in their place.

Change is only likely to happen when there are political circumstances that demand it. That probably means when there is an election which produces a hung parliament and the need for major parties to make concessions as the price of support from others. A hung parliament on its own, however, is not enough. Although the 2010 election did not give any party a clear majority, the political circumstances were such that the referendum won through the coalition negotiations stood very little chance of success – change was the project of a minor party, and with the opposition of the Conservatives, the Liberal Democrats' much larger coalition partner, and of many in Labour's ranks, it was doomed to failure.

How might circumstances arise that could lead to a change to TR? What we are likely to need are:

- Another hung parliament so that the smaller parties that want reform have leverage; and
- Strong support for change within at least one of the major parties

Another hung parliament is almost inevitable, and it may come sooner rather than later. Although many have support FPTP assuming that it will deliver strong, single-party government, the evidence suggests that they are wrong, and that 2010 was not just an aberration. When Britain was essentially a two-party system, whichever party won was likely to have an out-right majority in the Commons. But Britain is no longer a two-party system – in recent elections, the Conservatives and Labour have won only around two-thirds of the votes, and although they have won 86 – 87% of the seats, there were still 85 seats won by other parties in 2010. Thus for one of the two major parties to win an overall Commons majority, they not only need to defeat their main rival but need to do so by a margin that is greater than total seats won by these other parties. The more the smaller parties gain in strength, the more unlikely it is that we will see any one party winning outright.

There is of course speculation that the 2015 election will see the move away from two-party politics halted, or even reversed, through Liberal Democrat support being reduced by the bruising experience of having been a minor and troubled coalition partner. However, in the more pluralist politics we now have, there is clearly a space for a major, national third party and it would be a mistake to assume that the Liberal Democrats will be punished as much as some think. But even if the Liberal Democrats were to suffer a setback, there are two further factors to consider: the SNP made huge gains in the 2011 Scottish Parliament elections and may well win additional seats in the next general election, and the changes to constituency boundaries will introduce a new area of uncertainty. Thus while we cannot confidently predict a hung parliament after the next election, it nevertheless remains very possible, and even if that election does produce an outright winner, it cannot be long before we see parties again needing to negotiate another coalition. Such negotiations will almost certainly involve the Liberal Democrats, and given their treatment at the hands of FPTP, they would be foolish not to make some sort of electoral reform one of their demands.

When we do have another hung parliament, if we are to make progress in reforming the voting system it will be important to have one of the two major parties supporting change: if we do not, we risk a replay of 2010, i.e. an agreement to hold a referendum, but not enough agreement over the proposition that was put. AV with only half-hearted support by half of the Labour Party was never going to be enough for victory – it needed the strong support of one of the major parties if it was going to have a chance of winning.

At present that appears to mean Labour support. Over the years the Conservatives have been united and consistent in their opposition to any reform of the voting system and there is no indication that they are likely to change their position. If the next election were to lead to a Liberal Democrat-Labour coalition, it is therefore important that any proposal for electoral reform that emerges from the negotiations is seen not as a concession to the Liberal Democrats but as a Labour project that will be fully backed by Labour in any referendum. How this might be achieved is a question we will return to shortly.

The route to a referendum

There is no constitutional requirement for a referendum to change the voting system, but change without one would be difficult. Without a manifesto commitment, a proposal to make the change without a referendum would not just be regarded as bad form by many reformers at Westminster but would probably be blocked in the Lords. However, if a party were to win power with a commitment to change the system, then the Lords, assuming they follow the convention by which they do not vote against manifesto commitments, would not oppose it but, as an outright Liberal Democrat win is unlikely and as there appears little prospect of the Conservatives doing a U-turn on voting reform, it would require a commitment from Labour. Labour, however, has often stated that "A referendum is the right way to agree any change for Westminster".[22] We must therefore assume that any change to the voting system will only come about through a referendum.

Is it possible to win Labour's backing for reform in a new referendum? It is certainly not impossible. Labour did, after all, commit itself to a referendum on AV in its 2010 manifesto, and although it lost the election, when the referendum nevertheless came, most of Labour's leaders backed AV. If that referendum had been a Labour project, it is safe to assume that many more Labour supporters would have voted for change.

---

[22] Labour manifesto, 2001

Labour only decided in favour of a referendum when it was clear that it was heading for defeat. At that stage the promise of a referendum made it more likely that the Liberal Democrats would back Labour in the event of a hung parliament, and it was no doubt assumed that with the Liberal Democrats supporting Labour, AV would have been in Labour's interests in future elections.

Labour may find itself in a similar situation as the next general election approaches. In spite of the country's economic woes and the Conservative-led government's programme of cuts in services and benefits, Labour has not managed to establish a commanding lead over the Conservatives in the opinion polls, and certainly not the sort of lead it would need to give it an overall majority. Impending boundary changes may also remove some of the advantages Labour gets from FPTP, and Scottish independence (unlikely although it might be, particularly before 2015) would make an outright Labour victory exceptionally hard to achieve. As the 2015 election gets closer, Labour may well come to the conclusion that getting back into government will require Liberal Democrat support and, whatever they may think of electoral reform, the offer of a chance to change the voting system is politically necessary to gain that support.

Offering a referendum in 2015, however, might not be as straightforwards as it was in 2010. As the electorate rejected AV in 2011, any party promising another referendum – even if on TR rather than AV - would risk accusations that it is ignoring the voice of the people. Much more possible, however, would be a commitment to a process that could lead to a referendum on TR. How then do we get electoral reform back on the agenda?

One approach worth exploring is a 'citizens' assembly' or a 'constitutional convention' to examine the issue – an idea the government toyed with prior to the 2010 election. Here the best example to follow would be the 'Citizens' Assembly on Electoral Reform' set up by the British Columbia's provincial government. Having decided to hold a referendum on their voting system, in 2003 British Columbia formed their Assembly by selecting 160 electors at random, but in a way that ensured a man and a woman from each constituency and a range of ages. Those selected then met every other weekend for nearly a year, they toured the province to listen to what people wanted from their parliament, they received 1600 written submissions and they summoned expert witnesses. Almost unanimously they recommended STV. In the 2005 referendum that followed, 58% voted for change.

The story, however, does not have such a happy ending. As the government had decided that 60% would be needed to bring about change, a second referendum was held in 2009. That year, out-manoeuvred by the media campaign of those opposed to reform and without adequate backing from political parties, the change proposition lost heavily. The Assembly had had the merit of taking the decision on the voting system out of the hands of the politicians who had vested interests, but that was perhaps also its downfall. Whether we like it or not, politicians will play a big part, and will be influential, when it comes to any referendum. An

Assembly that included representatives from the political parties might not have produced such a radical proposal, and it might have produced a proposal with more political support.

This suggests that for the UK we should aim for an 'assembly' or 'convention' largely of randomly selected electors, but with representatives of the parties. Its remit could be:

1. To consider whether there is a case for changing the voting system;
2. If there is case, to recommend a system, which will be put to the electorate in a referendum, which is:
   • Fairer to parties and voters, but not necessarily proportional;
   • Is easy for voters to use;
   • Is easy to understand and transparent.

Of course there is a risk that such an assembly might not come up with the answers that reformers want, but if the argument for TR, or any other system, cannot be won through detailed and objective debate by a largely impartial body, then the argument is not likely to be won with the electorate at large. Here we must have faith in the merits of the change we want to see.

One advantage of the assembly approach is that the proposal put in the referendum comes from a body mainly composed of ordinary electors. If the referendum is the project of one or two political parties it is almost inevitable that other parties will oppose it, or at least find it hard to support, but it is much harder for politicians to oppose the considered recommendations of a non-partisan group of voters. Indeed, some have speculated that the 2005 referendum in British Columbia was won because the question was whether people accepted the recommendation of the Citizens' Assembly, while the 2009 referendum on whether people wanted STV was lost.

However, in the aftermath of the 2011 referendum, getting Labour, or any other party, to commit itself in its manifesto to a process that is just about electoral reform might be a problem. A way round this difficulty could be an assembly with a remit that includes looking at the voting system but which also takes on board some of the other unresolved constitutional issues – the nature and role of a reformed second chamber, how we deal with 'asymmetric devolution' and the role of Scottish MPs at Westminster, whether the voting age should be reduced to 16, etc. The referendum following the assembly's work would then need to pose a number of questions covering the assembly's recommendations. With such a broad mandate, there is of course a risk that the debate on the voting system, both within the assembly and in the referendum campaign period, might be diluted, but if such an assembly is the only way forwards then it is a risk worth taking.

The composition of an assembly and its manner of working would need a lot of discussion, but minimum requirements should be:

- The majority of its members should be ordinary electors chosen at random;

- The assembly should be sufficiently large to ensure it cannot be dominated by any particular group within it, and to allow representation from all parts of the UK and of all age groups; it should be gender-balanced and should include representatives of minority communities;
- Within its remit, the assembly should be free to set its own agenda;
- The assembly should be given sufficient time to take evidence from expert witnesses and others who wish to present their views, and time to deliberate on what it has heard;
- The assembly should have an impartial chair whose role would be to steer the process rather than lead the debate.

Thus some form of citizens' assembly or constitution convention may be a possible route, and may turn out to be the only route, to a referendum on TR (or on issues including TR). A more direct move to a referendum through an agreement between parties in the aftermath of an indecisive election, however, would be faster and avoid the risk of the assembly making (or being steered into) a less satisfactory recommendation.

Could a referendum be won?

Even if a proposal for electoral reform had Labour backing, victory could not be taken for granted. The AV referendum campaign demonstrated how easy it was for an anti-reform campaign to swing public opinion against change. The 'No' campaign may at times have been disingenuous, and even dishonest, but it was highly effective and a similar campaign could easily derail any future reform proposal. A Labour-supported campaign should not imply one that is opposed by the Conservatives, and proposing TR against the full force of the Conservative Party's electoral machine is something to be avoided if at all possible.

The nature of our party politics makes it unlikely that the Conservatives would enthusiastically support something Labour wants, but winning at least some support for TR within Conservative ranks should, fortunately, not be impossible. TR, unlike AV, would offer the Conservatives additional seats in Scotland, the North East and other areas where they are weak, and while TR is overall a fairer system than FPTP, it does not make it impossible for the Conservatives to win power on their own. TR's requirement for some boundary changes is perhaps the aspect of the system most vulnerable to attack but, having pushed in parliament for the most radical boundary changes in decades, it would be difficult for the Conservatives to mount a full-blown attack on this issue. Thus while a truly all-party campaign for TR might be too much to expect, there are grounds for hoping that TR would not face the onslaught of criticism from which AV suffered.

There will, however, always be opposition to change. Just as some saw AV, rightly or wrongly, as a threat, there will be some who oppose TR. However, as we have noted in earlier chapters, attacking TR would be harder to do – none could claim it makes voting difficult, and any suggestion that it would hugely increase the costs of elections would be absurd. While AV is a quite simple system, it proved hard to sell to the average elector, but the same problems are not as likely to arise with TR. When it comes to winning a referendum, TR is therefore likely to be a better bet.

Winning a referendum requires not just a good proposal but a good campaign that reaches all electors with messages meaningful to them. Here there are lessons to be learnt from the 2011 AV referendum, particularly on strategy and organisation.

Although the 2011 campaign has been criticised for relying too heavily on the activities of local supporters around the country, electoral reformers are nevertheless likely to be the foot soldiers of any reform campaign. While they might not be able to win votes on the scale a referendum requires, a campaign without local champions would find the going hard, and the opposition of significant numbers of electoral reformers would be a gift to any anti-TR campaign. Winning the support of the reform lobby is therefore important.

Here, however, there are grounds for cautious optimism. TR is not STV and it would not bring about the radical changes that most electoral reformers would like to see – to some for whom proportional representation is the ultimate objective, TR might appear at best a sell-out and at worst heresy. Nevertheless, the great majority of reformers want change, and if TR offers them the best chance of getting it they are likely to give support. Just as most of those who denounced AV and demanded proportional representation in the pre-2010 period rolled up their sleeves to work for AV, if TR were the option on the table there is every reason to expect most reformers to do what is needed of them. As TR is a newcomer to the debate, however, a big educational job would be needed.

Thus there is every reason to believe that a referendum campaign on TR could succeed and would not suffer the fate of that on AV.

Fixing our broken democracy

CHAPTER 11

In conclusion

Just because one attempt to change our voting system has been defeated is no reason to allow electoral reform to drop off the agenda. Politicians might argue that with the country's economic problems they have more important things to talk about, but what can be more important than ensuring we have the right people and a democratically legitimate government deciding how we respond to any crisis? The rejection of AV does not make FPTP any better, and if there were reasons for demanding a change in the system before May 2011 then there are just as many reasons for demanding change now.

The only thing that is new is the appearance on the scene of TR – a system that offers greater fairness to voters by taking account of more votes in determining the outcome of elections, and greater fairness to parties without moving all the way to proportionality. It does this without requiring any changes in the way people vote, thereby making it less vulnerable to the sort of attacks that were AV's downfall.

Electoral reformers have always assumed that a hung parliament would provide the opportunity for pro-reform parties to demand change. The 2010 general election produced a hung parliament, but the resulting referendum on a rather unsatisfactory reform was a failure. There is every reason to believe, however, that another opportunity, through another hung parliament or the expectation on one, will arise before long. Another referendum, with a better campaign and TR as the question, would be winnable.

TR, we have argued, is a voting system that would work for general elections in the UK, as well as for local elections in those parts of the country that still use FPTP. The changes it would make to our elections are not radical, but would nevertheless be significant. Modelling how general elections might have looked, even accepting the limitations of using votes cast under one system to predict what might have happened under another, demonstrate that the broad shape of electoral outcomes would have remained the same, but the results would have better reflected the support received by the parties. There would have been little change in the relative strengths of the Conservatives and Labour, but the Liberal Democrats would not have been so disadvantaged as they would have been under FPTP and smaller parties, particularly UKIP which got nothing from near a million votes in 2010, would have had representation.

The model of TR we have used – one party seat for every five constituencies and party seats allocated in the existing regions – was chosen taking account of the political considerations and the opposition to further boundary changes that might be encountered. However, it is not the only approach that might have been used, and a higher ratio of party seats would have been fairer, and possibly better, in the long-run.

Assessing TR as voting system, however, should not be just a matter of deciding what is politically desirable and feasible at one point in the development of a country's democracy. TR comes with a philosophy. It is based on the idea that just because a voter does not support the winning candidate in a constituency, his or her views should not just be ignored. Votes for losing candidates are nevertheless votes – expressions of what electors want – and it is reasonable that the outcome of an election should take some account of their views. In that sense TR is indeed 'total representation': it seeks representation based on the totality of electors' views.

Some may argue that the name 'Total Representation' claims too much for the system – with TR there will be some votes that count for nothing (but that is the case with all voting systems) and much more weight is given to votes for constituency winners than votes for losers. While there is perhaps a case for a debate over the name, what is important is not the name but the essence of TR – the way that account is taken of votes that under FPTP would simply have been wasted. With the simple innovation, Aharon Nathan has given those who design voting systems a powerful new tool.

This book has been about the changes that are needed in British democracy. TR, however, offers advantages for other countries as well. Anywhere that single-member constituencies are used, or where a change to single-member constituencies is being considered, TR is an option which should be on the table. Others may want to modify it or adapt it – just as Thomas Hare's innovation of transferable votes was converted into STV – and where the political culture is more conducive to broad proportionality, a higher ratio of party to constituency seats than has here been advocated for the UK might be considered. In Israel, where a debate on electoral reform is already underway, the late Professor Gideon Doren, while President of the Israel Political Science Association, wrote:

> "John Stuart Mill ... expressed his opinion that Thomas Hare's STV system was 'one of the greatest improvements in the theory and practice of voting methods': I think no less of Aharon Nathan's invention of TR".

Professor Ivo Skrabalo has also written of the possible use of TR for Croatia and, as more countries become aware of its potential, more are likely to consider it as an electoral option.

Here, however, we are concerned with the UK. TR is a system around which both electoral reformers and those wary of radical change could unite – a system that could break FPTP's centuries-old stranglehold on British democracy and usher in a new era of fairer elections and more representative government. Aharon Nathan has given us the means – now it's up to those of us who want a better form of politics in Britain to make the change.

Appendix 1

Modelling the 2010 General Election using TR

This appendix gives a picture of what the 2010 General Election might have looked like if TR had been used instead of FPTP. As noted in chapter 8, however, there are different ways in which TR might be applied and we have therefore modelled the election using a number of different assumptions.

Part A assumes the use of the 650 constituencies used in 2010 and a ratio of 1:5 (i.e. one party seat for every 5 constituencies) to see how TR might have affected the outcome. We look at what the outcome would have been if party seats had been allocated:

- Regionally (using the administrative regions that are used for European Parliament elections);
- Regionally/sub-regionally, dividing regions of more than 50 constituencies into two sub-regions, each of at least 25 constituencies, and the South East (which has 83 constituencies) into three.

These modelled results, however, are presented only to demonstrate how TR might work. As discussed in chapter 8, when the Commons is about to move from 650 to 600 seats, a change to 780 seats (650 constituency seats and 130 party seats) would clearly not be politically acceptable.

Part B assumes that the size of the Commons is reduced to 600 seats (constituency plus party seats) and that party seats are allocated regionally. It also compares the outcomes if the ratios of party to constituency seats were 1:4, 1:5 and 1:6.

Firstly, however, some cautionary remarks are needed on the assumptions we have made. In modelling past elections with TR we cannot state with any certainly what the outcomes would have been because:

1. some voters might have voted differently: if they knew their votes could help win party seats they might have voted sincerely (i.e. for their preferred candidates) rather than tactically;
2. some who did not vote might have felt more inclined to vote if they had known their votes were not going to be wasted.

Nevertheless, we will assume that votes cast under TR would have been the same as votes in the actual FPTP elections – that should give us a reasonable picture of what the results with TR might have been, although in looking at modelled results we must remember that with TR voters might have been treated small parties more generously.

Part A

Modelling the 2010 General Election using TR assuming

- **Existing (2010) constituencies:**
- **Party seats allocated regionally and regionally/sub-regionally**
- **A ratio of one party seat for every 5 constituencies (with the number of party seats rounded where necessary).**

ENGLAND

Eastern England

	%age vote	Const seats	Party seats	Total seats	*Total seats*
			Regional allocation		*Sub-region alloc.**
Conservative	47.1	52	1	53	*52*
Labour	19.6	2	4	6	*6*
Lib Democrat	24.1	4	5	9	*10*
UKIP	4.3	0	1	1	*2*
BNP	2.1	0	1	1	*0*
Green	1.5	0	0	0	*0*

*Region divided East-West

East Midlands

	%age vote	Const seats	Party seats	Total seats	Total seats
		Regional allocation			Sub-region alloc.*
Conservative	41.2	31	1	32	32
Labour	29.8	15	3	18	18
Lib Democrat	20.8	0	3	3	3
UKIP	3.3	0	1	1	1
BNP	3.1	0	1	1	1
Green	0.5	0	0	0	0

Region not subdivided as only 48 constituencies

London

	%age vote	Const seats	Party seats	Total seats	Total seats
		Regional allocation			Sub-region alloc.*
Conservative	34.5	28	5	33	33
Labour	36.6	38	3	41	42
Lib Democrat	22.1	7	5	12	12
UKIP	1.7	0	1	1	0
BNP	1.5	0	0	0	0
Green	1.6	0	1	1	0

Region divided North and South of Thames

North East

	%age vote	Const seats	Party seats	Total seats	Total seats
		Regional allocation			Sub-region alloc.*
Conservative	23.7	2	2	4	4
Labour	43.6	25	1	26	26
Lib Democrat	23.6	2	2	4	4
UKIP	2.7	0	0	0	0
BNP	4.4	0	1	1	1
Green	0.3	0	0	0	0

Region not divided

North West

	%age vote	Const seats	Party seats	Total seats	Total seats
		Regional allocation			Sub-region alloc.*
Conservative	31.7	22	5	27	27
Labour	39.4	47	3	50	50
Lib Democrat	21.6	6	5	11	11
UKIP	3.2	0	1	1	2
BNP	2.1	0	1	1	0
Green	0.5	0	0	0	0

Region divided West/North, and East

South East

	%age vote	Const seats	Party seats	Total seats	_Total seats_
			Regional allocation		_Sub-region alloc.*_
Conservative	49.3	75	1	76	_75_
Labour	16.2	4	5	9	_8_
Lib Democrat	26.2	4	8	12	_13_
UKIP	4.1	0	2	2	_3_
BNP	0.7	0	0	0	_0_
Green	1.4	1	1	2	_1_

Region divided in three: North, South West and South East

South West

	%age vote	Const seats	Party seats	Total seats	_Total seats_
			Regional allocation		_Sub-region alloc.*_
Conservative	42.8	36	3	39	_38_
Labour	15.4	4	3	7	_7_
Lib Democrat	34.7	15	4	19	_19_
UKIP	4.8	0	1	1	_2_
BNP	1.1	0	0	0	_0_
Green	0.7	0	0	0	_0_

Region divided East and West

West Midlands

	%age votes	Const seats	Party seats	Total seats	*Total seats*
			Regional allocation		Sub-region alloc.*
Conservative	39.3	33	3	36	*36*
Labour	30.7	24	3	27	*27*
Lib Democrat	20.7	2	4	6	*6*
UKIP	4.0	0	1	1	*2*
BNP	2.7	0	1	1	*0*
Green	0.6	0	0	0	*0*

*Region divided Birmingham/Wolverhampton/W Brom area, and Other

Yorkshire and Humberside

	%age Votes	Const seats	Party seats	Total seats	*Total seats*
			Regional allocation		Sub-region alloc.*
Conservative	32.8	19	3	22	*22*
Labour	34.4	32	2	34	*34*
Lib Democrat	22.9	3	4	7	*7*
UKIP	2.8	0	1	1	*0*
BNP	4.3	0	1	1	*2*
Green	0.9	0	0	0	*0*

*Region divided North South

SCOTLAND

	%age votes	Const seats	Party seats	Total seats	*Total seats*
		Regional allocation			*Sub-region alloc.**
Conservative	16.8	1	4	5	*5*
Labour	42.0	41	1	42	*42*
Lib Democrat	18.9	11	3	14	*13*
SNP	19.9	6	4	10	*11*
UKIP	0.7	0	0	0	*0*
BNP	0.4	0	0	0	*0*
Green	0.7	0	0	0	*0*

Divided North/East and Glasgow and SW

WALES

	%age votes	Const seats	Party seats	Total seats	*Total seats*
		Regional allocation			*Sub-region alloc.**
Conservative	26.1	8	3	11	*11*
Labour	36.2	26	1	27	*27*
Lib Democrat	20.1	3	2	5	*5*
Plaid	11.3	3	1	4	*4*
UKIP	2.4	0	1	1	*1*
BNP	1.6	0	0	0	*0*
Green	0.4	0	0	0	*0*

Wales not sub-divided

NORTHERN IRELAND

	%age votes	Regional allocation			Sub-region alloc.*
		Const it seats	Party seats	Total seats	Total seats
Alliance	6.3	1	0	1	1
Con & Unionist	15.2	0	1	1	1
DUP	25.0	8	1	9	9
SDLP	16.5	3	1	4	4
Sinn Fein	25.5	5	1	6	6
Independent	6.5	1	n.a.	1	1

*N Ireland not sub-divided

UK TOTAL

		Regional allocation.			Sub-region alloc
Conservative	36.1	307	31	338	335
Labour	29.0	258	29	287	287
Lib Democrat	23.0	57	45	102	103
UKIP	3.1	0	10	10	13
BNP	1.9	0	6	6	4
Green	1.0	1	2	3	1
SNP	1.7	6	4	10	11
Plaid	0.6	3	1	4	4
N Ireland Parties	2.3	18	4	22	22
Other	1.3	0	0	0	0
TOTAL		650	132	782	780

Constituencies in which losing candidates would have won Party Seats

Constituencies are listed in descending order of the votes (actual rather than share of the votes) for the parties' candidates in the constituencies. The numbers of constituencies shown relates to the numbers of party seats won under regional allocation.

Region	Party	Constituencies
East England	Con	Norfolk North
	Lab	Waveney, Thurrock, Ipswich, Bedford
	Lib Dem	Cambridgeshire SE, Cambridgeshire S, Chelmsford, St Albans, Watford
	UKIP	Cambridgeshire NW
	BNP	Thurrock
East Midlands	Con	Gedling
	Lab	Corby, Broxtowe, Sherwood
	Lib Dem	Bosworth, Chesterfield, Harborough
	UKIP	Boston and Skegness
	BNP	Leicestershire NW
London	Con	Kingston and Sutton, Sutton and Cheam, Twickenham, Tooting, Hampstead and Kilburn
	Lab	Hendon, Hornsey and Wood Green, Brent Central
	Lib Dem	Richmond Park, Streatham, Hampstead and Kilburn, Holborn and St Pancras, Islington S and Finsbury
	UKIP	Hornchurch and Upminster
North East	Con	Tynemouth, Middlesborough S and Cleveland E

	Lab	Stockton S
	Lib Dem	City of Durham, Newcastle-upon-Tyne N
	BNP	Jarrow
North West	Con	Cheadle, Chorley, Westmorland and Lonsdale, Bolton W, Lancashire W
	Lab	Manchester Withington, Warrington S, S Ribble
	Lib Dem	Congleton, Rochdale, Warrington S, Oldham E and Saddleworth, Liverpool Wavertree
	UKIP	Ribble Valley
	BNP	Burnley
South East	Con	Eastbourne
	Lab	Hastings and Rye, Milton Keynes S, Dover, Hove, Crawley
	Lib Dem	Winchester, Oxford W and Abington, Isle of Wight, Guildford, Sussex Mid, Newbury, Romsey and Southampton N, Woking
	UKIP	Buckingham, Spelthorne
	Green	Hove
South West	Con	Somerton and Frome, Devon W and Torridge, Taunton and Deane
	Lab	Stroud, Gloucester, Kingswood
	Lib Dem	Dorset W, Devon W and Torridge, Somerset W, Weston-Super-Mare
	UKIP	Devon E
West Midlands	Con	Solihull, Birmingham Edgbaston, Coventry S
	Lab	Warwickshire N, Warwick and Leamington, Stafford

	Lib Dem	Worcestershire W, Hereford and Herefordshire S, Ludlow, Shrewsbury and Atcham
	UKIP	Staffordshire Moorlands
	BNP	West Bromwich W
Yorks & Humber	Con	Morley and Outwood, Batley and Spen, Wakefield
	Lab	Elmet and Rothwell, Dewsbury
	Lib Dem	Harrowgate and Knaresborough, York Outer, Skipton and Rippon, Sheffield Central
	UKIP	Wentworth and Dearne
	BNP	Rotherham
Scotland	Con	Berwick Roxburgh and Selkirk, Dumfries and Galloway, Renfrewshire E, Perth and N Perthshire
	Lab	Dunbarton E
	Lib Dem	Dunfermline and Fife W, Edinburgh N and Leith, Edinburgh S, Aberdeen S
	SNP	Falkirk, Ochil and S Perthshire, Linlithgow and Falkirk W, Livingston
Wales	Con	Brecon and Radnorshire, Gower, Alyn and Deeside
	Lab	Cardiff N
	Lib Dem	Montgomeryshire, Swansea W
	Plaid	Llanelli
	UKIP	Vale of Glamorgan
Northern Ireland	Con & Unionist	Upper Bann
	DUP	Belfast E
	SDLP	Newry and Armagh
	Sinn Fein	Belfast N

Part B

Modelling the 2010 General Election using TR assuming

- **A total of 600 seats**
- **Party seats allocated regionally**
- **Party to constituency seat ratios of 1:4, 1:5 and 1:6**

Here we look at the 2010 election using more likely scenarios for general elections given the decision to reduce the size of the Commons to 600 seats. The target numbers of seats used in modelling were:

Ratio	Constituencies	Party seats	Total seats
1:4	480	120	600
1:5	500	100	600
1:6	515	85	600

In the actual modelling, however, the totals differ by one seat from those shown above because of rounding to give an integral number of constituency seats and party seats in each region, resulting in totals of 599 for the ratios 1:4 and 1:5.

In addition to the limitations of modelling noted in the introduction to this appendix, here there is a further approximation we need to make in reducing the numbers of constituencies won by the different parties from 650 to the numbers required by the models. It has been assumed that in the reduction of constituency numbers all parties are affected in the same way. For example, in the 2010 election, the Conservatives won 307 of the 650 seats, which is 47.2%. Using TR with only 600 seats in total and a ratio of 1:4, there would have been 480 constituencies and 120 party seats. It has therefore been assumed that the Conservatives would have won 47.2% of the 480 constituencies which, when rounded, is 227. In practice, of course, boundary changes are likely to produce winners and losers but, for the purposes of illustration, this seems to be a reasonable assumption to make.

Within each region it has been assumed that the number of votes cast for each party would have been the same as in the actual election, and that for each party the numbers of votes for winning candidates and for losers would have been the same – again, an approximation but a reasonable one for our purposes.

Party seats per region have been calculated by applying the appropriate ratio to the reduced number of seats. Eastern Region, for example, had 58 constituencies in 2010, but reducing the total number of seats from 650 to 480 to achieve a ratio of 1:4, it would only have been entitled to 58 x (480/650), which is 42.83. Dividing 42.83 by 4 gives 10.7, which rounds to 11.

This leads to the following results:

	1:4			1:5			1:6		
	Const	Party	Total	Const	Party	Total	Const	Party	Total
Con	227	28	255	236	24	260	243	22	265
Lab	191	26	217	198	22	220	204	18	222
Lib Dem	42	43	85	44	36	80	45	32	77
SNP	4	4	8	5	3	8	5	3	8
Plaid	2	1	3	2	1	3	2	1	3
Green	1	2	3	1	0	1	1	0	1
UKIP	0	8	8	0	7	7	0	5	5
BNP	0	4	4	3	0	3	0	3	3
N Ire[23]	13	3	16	14	3	17	14	2	16
	480	119	599	500	99	599	514	86	600

Converting the total number of seats in each into percentage terms gives a clearer picture of how they compare with the actual 2010 result:

	FPTP (actual)	1:4	1:5	1:6
		TR		
Con	47.2	42.6	43.4	44.2
Lab	39.7	36.2	36.7	37.0
Lib Dem	8.8	14.2	13.4	12.8
SNP	0.9	1.3	1.3	1.3
Plaid	0.5	0.5	0.5	0.5
Green	0.2	0.5	0.2	0.2
UKIP	0.0	1.3	1.2	0.8
BNP	0.0	0.7	0.5	0.5
N Ire	2.8	2.7	2.8	2.7

---

[23] I.e. total for all those elected in Northern Ireland.

What we see is that:

- TR would only have reduced the Conservative lead over Labour very slightly;

- The Liberal Democrats would have gained most with TR, although their share of the seats would be far from the 23% of the votes they received;

- Although TR with a ratio of 1:4 should be more proportional as there are more party seats to be allocated, whether 1:4, 1:5 or 1:6 had been used would not have greatly affected the positions of the major parties;

- A ratio of 1:4, as might have been expected, would have given the smaller parties more seats.

Appendix 2

Modelling past general elections with TR

This appendix looks at how TR might have affected the results of general elections from 1992 to 2005.

For each election, however, the number of constituencies has been reduced to 600 (the number proposed for 2015 and future elections). A ratio of one party seat for every 5 constituencies has been used and party seats have been allocated regionally. The approach taken is the same as was used in Appendix 1 (Part B).

2005

	FPTP actual	FPTP adjusted	Party seats	TR total seats	%age vote	% FPTP seats	% TR seats
Con	198	153	30	182	32.4%	30.7%	30.6%
Lab	356	276	22	297	35.2%	55.1%	49.7%
Lib Dem	62	48	35	82	22.1%	9.6%	13.9%
UKIP	0		4	4	2.2%	0.0%	0.7%
BNP	0		1	1	0.7%	0.0%	0.2%
Green	0		1	1	1.0%	0.0%	0.2%
SNP	6	5	2	7	1.5%	0.9%	1.2%
Plaid	3	2	1	3	0.6%	0.5%	0.5%
N Ireland	18	14	3	17	2.6%	2.8%	2.8%
Other	3	2	0	2	1.7%	0.5%	0.3%
TOTAL	646	500	96	599			

This was an election that gave Labour a comfortable majority on only 35% of the votes. These figures suggest that with TR Labour might have just failed to gain a Commons majority (although we cannot be certain because of the limitations on modelling we have referred to earlier), and as Labour had not much more than a third of the votes this would have been a fairer outcome. Labour would, however, have had a clear lead over the Conservatives and the Liberal Democrats combined, and with TR the election would probably still have led to a Labour government.

2001

	FPTP actual	FPTP adjusted	Party seats	TR total seats	%age vote	% FPTP seats	% TR seats
Con	166	126	38	164	40.7%	25.2%	27.4%
Lab	413	313	19	332	31.7%	62.7%	55.4%
Lib Dem	52	39	32	71	18.3%	7.9%	11.9%
UKIP	0	0	2	2	1.5%	0.0%	0.3%
BNP	0	0	0	0	0.2%	0.0%	0.0%
Green	0	0	1	1	0.6%	0.0%	0.2%
SNP	5	4	3	7	1.8%	0.8%	1.2%
Plaid	4	3	1	4	0.7%	0.6%	0.7%
N Ireland	18	14	3	17	3.1%	2.7%	2.8%
Other	1	1	0	1	1.4%	0.2%	0.2%
TOTAL	659	500	99	599			

In 2001 Labour had a convincing win, and while with TR its majority would have been reduced, it would still have been a clear winner.

1997

	FPTP actual	FPTP adjusted	Party seats	TR total seats	%age vote	% FPTP seats	% TR seats
Con	165	125	39	164	30.7%	25.0%	27.3%
Lab	419	318	19	337	43.2%	63.6%	56.2%
Lib Dem	46	35	29	64	16.8%	7.0%	10.7%
SNP	6	5	3	8	2.0%	0.9%	1.3%
Plaid	4	3	1	4	0.5%	0.6%	0.7%
Ref Party	0	0	5	5	2.6%	0.0%	0.8%
N Ireland	18	14	3	17	2.3%	2.7%	2.8%
Other	1	1	0	1	1.9%	0.2%	0.2%
TOTAL	659	501	99	600			

This was the year that Labour ended 18 years of Conservative government with a 'landslide' win. Its 63.6% of the seats, however, was gained with only 43.3% of the votes. With TR Labour would still have had a formidable majority, but not such an exaggerated one as with FPTP.

1992

	FPTP actual	FPTP adjusted	Party seats	TR total seats	%age vote	% FPTP seats	% TR seats
Con	336	258	28	286	41.9%	51.5%	47.7%
Lab	271	208	29	237	34.4%	41.6%	39.6%
Lib Dem	20	15	35	50	17.8%	3.1%	8.3%
SNP	3	2	3	5	1.9%	0.5%	0.8%
Plaid	4	3	1	4	0.5%	0.6%	0.7%
N Ireland	18	14	3	17	2.2%	2.8%	2.8%
Other	0	0	0	0	1.3%	0.0%	0.0%
TOTAL	652	500	99	599			

In 1992 Labour had hoped for better, but John Major's Conservatives had a narrow win. With TR, their 41.9% of the votes would not have been enough for a majority, but a Labour-Liberal Democrat coalition would not have had a majority either. Whether TR would have led to a minority Conservative government, or a coalition government (possibly a minority Labour-Liberal Democrat one) is difficult to say, but it is unlikely that it would have produced a government that would have lasted 5 years.

Appendix 3

Modelling local elections using TR

Chapter 9 looked at how TR might be used for local elections in England and Wales. Three local authorities were considered – Camden and Kingston in London, and Birmingham. This appendix gives more detailed results of modelling for these councils.

All three at present use three-member wards. It is assumed that TR would be applied using existing ward boundaries, but with each three-member ward electing just two members by FPTP and a third of the seats being party seats. In each case the local authority areas have been divided into subdistricts and party seats allocated within the subdistricts.

Using TR in this way, each voter would have just two votes instead of three. Using the 2010 local elections, in each ward it has been assumed that where a party had three candidates under FPTP, under TR the party's two candidates would have been those with the highest numbers of votes (and that the votes they would have received would have been the same as under FPTP). Clearly votes may have differed if TR had been used, but the assumption is a reasonable one for the purposes of illustration.

With TR small parties would have much more incentive to stand candidates in all wards – even if they had no realistic chance of winning, the votes they receive could help their party gain party seats. Where a party had candidates in at least half of the wards in a subdistrict, it has been assumed that under TR it would have stood two candidates in each ward. Where parties did not stand a candidate (or only stood one), it is likely that they felt support for the party (or for a second candidate) would be low. The extra candidates added for modelling have therefore been given 90% of the lowest number of votes received by any of those parties' candidates in the subdistrict. This is of course just a guesstimate, but one that makes little difference to the outcomes.

The two London boroughs elect all their councillors every four years, but Birmingham uses elections 'in thirds' (i.e. electing one councillor in each ward in three years out of every four). With TR it has been assumed that Birmingham would have four-yearly 'all out' elections and that both of a party's candidates in a ward would receive the same number of votes as cast for the single candidate in 2010.

The following tables show the modelled results by ward.

LONDON BOROUGH OF KINGSTON

		FPTP seats				TR seats			
		Con	Lab	LD	Grn	Con	Lab	LD	Grn
COOMBE	Coombe Hill	3				2			
AND	Coombe Vale	3				2			
MALDEN	Beverley			3				2	
	St James	3				2			
	Old Malden	3				2			
	Party seats					1	1	2	1
	TOTAL COOMBE / MALDEN	12	0	3	0	9	1	4	1
KINGSTON	Tudor	3				2			
TOWN	Canbury	2		1		1		1	
	Norbiton			3				2	
	Grove			3				2	
	St Marks			3				2	
	Berrylands	1		2				2	
	Party seats					3	1	1	1
	TOTAL KINGSTON TOWN	6	0	12		6	1	10	1
KINGSTON	Surbiton Hill			3				2	
SOUTH	Alexandra	2		1		1		1	
	Tolworth and Hook Rise			3				2	
	Chessington N and Hook	1		2				2	
	Chessington South			3				2	
	Party seats					3	1		1
	TOTAL KINGSTON SOUTH	3	0	12		4	1	9	1
KINGSTON	**TOTAL**	**21**	**0**	**27**		**19**	**3**	**23**	**3**

LONDON BOROUGH OF CAMDEN

		FPTP seats				TR seats			
		Con	Lab	LD	Grn	Con	Lab	LD	Grn
NORTH	Cantelowes		2	1			2		
	Gospel Oak		3				2		
	Hampstead Town	2		1		1		1	
	Haverstock			3				2	
	Highgate		2		1		1		1
	Kentish Town		3				2		
	Party seats					2	1	2	1
	TOTAL NORTH	2	10	5	1	3	8	5	2
WEST	Belsize	2		1		2			
	Fortune Green			3				2	
	Frognal and Fitzjohns	3				2			
	Kilburn		3				2		
	Swiss Cottage	3				2			
	West Hampstead			3				2	
	Party seats					1	2	2	1
	TOTAL WEST	8	3	7		7	4	6	1
SOUTH	Bloomsbury		3				2		
	Camden Town/Primrose H		2	1			1	1	
	Holborn & Covent Gdn		3				2		
	King's Cross		3				2		
	Regent's Park		3				2		
	St Pancras & Somers Town		3				2		
	Party seats					2		3	1
	TOTAL SOUTH		17	1		2	11	4	1
CAMDEN	**TOTAL**	**10**	**30**	**13**	**1**	**12**	**23**	**15**	**4**

186

BIRMINGHAM	FPTP seats (modelled)						TR seats					
NORTH	Con	Lab	LD	BNP	Grn	Rpt	Con	Lab	LD	BNP	Grn	Rpct
Sutton Four Oaks	3						2					
Sutton New Hall	3						2					
Sutton Trinity	3						2					
Sutton Vesey	3						2					
Tyburn		3						2				
Oscott		3						2				
Kingstanding		3						2				
Erdington	3						2					
Hodge Hill		3						2				
Shard End		3						2				
Party seats							2	3	3	1	1	
TOTAL NORTH	15	15	0	0	0	0	12	13	3	1	1	0

West & Central	Con	Lab	LD	BNP	Grn	Rpt	Con	Lab	LD	BNP	Grn	Rpct
Aston		3						2				
Handsworth Wood		3						2				
Ladywood		3						2				
Lozells & E Handsworth		3						2				
Nechells		3						2				
Perry Barr			3						2			
Soho		3						2				
Washwood Heath		3						2				
Bordesley Green		3						2				
Stockland Green		3						2				
Party seats							3	1	5		1	
TOTAL WEST AND CENTRAL	0	27	3	0	0	0	3	19	7	0	1	

Fixing our broken democracy

South East	FPTP seats (modelled)						TR seats					
	Con	Lab	LD	BNP	Grn	Rpt	Con	Lab	LD	BNP	Grn	Rspct
Billesley		3						2				
Brandwood		3						2				
Hall Green			3						2			
Moseley & Kings Heath			3						2			
Sheldon			3						2			
South Yardley			3						2			
Sparkbrook						3						2
Springfield		3						2				
Stechford & Yardley N			3						2			
Acocks Green			3						2			
Party seats							3	3	1	1	1	1
TOTAL SOUTH EAST	0	9	18	0	0	3	3	9	13	1	1	3

South West	Con	Lab	LD	BNP	Grn	Rpt	Con	Lab	LD	BNP	Grn	Rspct
Bartley Green	3						2					
Bournville	3						2					
Edgbaston	3						2					
Harborne	3						2					
Kings Norton		3						2				
Northfield	3						2					
Quinton		3						2				
Selly Oak			3						2			
Weoley	3						2					
Longbridge		3						2				
Party seats							2	4	2	1	1	
TOTAL SOUTH WEST	18	9	3	0	0	0	14	10	4	1	1	

| BIRMINGHAM TOTAL | 33 | 60 | 24 | | | 3 | 32 | 51 | 27 | 3 | | 4 |